Flywheels and Feedback Loops:

A Guide to Success for
Amazon Private-Label Sellers
First Edition

By Bernie Thompson
With Joni Sensel

Efficient Era
http://efficientera.com

This book is not intended as a substitute for common sense, having a clue, buying a vowel, or a thorough reading of Amazon policies and contractual agreements and those of other online marketplaces, not to mention applicable laws. It reflects the hard-won insights and experience of the author, but marketplace conditions and rules can change very rapidly, and your mileage may vary. The reader should consult with other trusted experts, as well as legal and financial professionals, and avoid doing anything foolish just because this guide may seem to suggest it.

ISBN: 978-0-9981211-2-3

Names: Thompson, Bernie, author | Sensel, Joni, author.
Title: Flywheels and Feedback Loops: A Guide to Success for Amazon Private-Label Sellers/Bernie Thompson with Joni Sensel
Description: First edition. | Seattle, Washington: Efficient Era, 2016
Subjects: Business, e-commerce, entrepreneurship, manufacturing, online marketplaces, Amazon
BISAC: BUS090000, Business & Economics > Ecommerce > General

For review copies or excerpt permission, or to be notified about new editions of this guide, please contact:

Efficient Era
http://efficientera.com/flywheels
flywheels@efficientera.com

Acknowledgements

Thanks to the following Efficient Era team members for their contributions and assistance, without which this book couldn't exist:

Ritu Java
David "Q" Quesenberry
Stephen McCray
Bruce Oliver
Jaimee Parker
Charlotte Young

Special thanks to Ritu for her many contributions and edits while guiding this book to completion, and to David for his keyword and Sponsored Advertising expertise.

First Edition

This guide is a snapshot of current best practices and advice for succeeding as a private-label seller in a dynamic, technology-based marketplace. We plan to update it frequently as our experience grows and conditions change. Check efficientera.com/flywheels for information about the latest edition.

Foreword

by Chris McCabe, CEO, ecommerceChris.com

As one of Amazon's first private label sellers, Bernie Thompson understands that selling on Amazon leaves no room for "wind it up and let it go" scenarios. Each seller must treat their account as a daily endeavor to make the most of all viable tools for success. You must have a keen grasp of both tools and Amazon's vision for the marketplace. Ultimately, this understanding vaulted Bernie from a new seller to ranking as one of the top Amazon sellers in the USA. His book, *Flywheels and Feedback Loops* will get you from the bottom to the top in short order, using approaches that sellers cannot afford to bypass.

Proactive and proven tips will help you manage your relationship with an unwieldy beast that functions both as partner and competitor. Without a solid awareness of Amazon's methodology and an interest in productively managing your side of their equation, you'll find it more and more difficult to navigate Amazon's increasingly complex universe. As a former Amazonian, performance and policy team member, and consultant to Amazon marketplace sellers, I've seen just about every mistake there is. I can attest to the fact that each error represents not only a lost business opportunity but an added risk that no seller should allow.

A healthy and growing Amazon marketplace account requires knowledge and proficiency in multiple key areas, but none are as important as this: Understand the kind of seller that Amazon wants to provide for its buyers and seek out as many opportunities as you can to achieve that ideal profile. Comprehend Amazon's vision for a seamless e-commerce buyer experience, where customers no longer need several back and forth interactions to get what they expect from a purchase. Amazon enforcement around compliance with policy will get tougher as the marketplace continues to grow, but knowing how to prepare and which tools to use will aid you considerably. In theory, this means being on your toes all the time and never letting your guard down. In practice, it means paying constant attention to the most efficient methods of listing products, the best implementation of an Amazon-styled customer service approach, and an obsessive focus on how to maximize your potential while playing by the rules.

What does this specifically require from you as a seller? As *Flywheels* explains quite clearly, mastering all changes to Amazon policies is essential. Sellers must be perfectly clear on the right and wrong ways to solicit reviews from buyers of your products, for example. Overall, you'll need to interpret bad product reviews, buyer comments, negative feedback, or claims as immediate warning signs. Action must be taken to make sure the same problem does not happen again. You'll need to consider additional due diligence measures such as more regular inspections of inventory, critical reviews of your supplier relationships, and greater involvement in your Quality Control processes. Anything less spells heartache in the long run, well beyond the friction you might feel from one or two bad product reviews or bad order experiences.

Consider also how often or accurately you respond to buyer requests for more information. Buyers want to know you're attentive to their needs, whether it's a product query before they buy or a request for help after something's gone wrong. Are you going to be there for an Amazon buyer, no matter what the situation? Are you sure you know exactly how to reply in each use case? If not, then professional advice from marketplace experts will fill in the gaps and move you along the path towards optimum account performance. *Flywheels* offers the chance to hone in on the best techniques.

Without the right means to execute best practices and expand your presence on Amazon, you run the risk of languishing in the background while your competition steps up. If you fail to appreciate the value of automated processes, the crucial importance of browse node and keyword use in search terms, or any new approach to competing for sales ahead of us, then you'll find a rough ride in front of you. Take time to accumulate knowledge and make the right decisions now, before you find yourself missing opportunities to optimize sales or even to comply with all of Amazon's policies for sellers. Getting reinstated from a suspension is harder now than it ever has been in the past, and suffering through lost sales of your top ASINs, let alone an entire account shutdown, is not a situation you want to know from personal experience.

Chris McCabe knows Amazon from the inside out, and as an Amazon expert is often quoted in CNBC, Bloomberg, and the Seattle Times. As the CEO of ecommercechris.com, he shows his clients how to think like Amazon. He spent several years at Amazon, evaluating seller account performance. Now he uses his insider knowledge to help sellers protect their accounts. He founded frustrationfreeamazon.com so you can learn the exact, proven strategy he uses to craft Amazon appeals and plans of action.

Efficient Era

Introduction:
Competing in Amazon's New Retail Era

Wow, has retailing changed! Online marketplaces such as Amazon have completely reinvented the way manufacturers get products to market.

Small manufacturers and brands can now sell directly to consumers globally, with Amazon providing all the logistics.

This isn't the first time retailing has changed drastically. The mom-and-pop corner store was outdone by the standardization and scale of the chain store. Then the largest of the big box stores such as Wal-Mart drove the supply chain global in search of lower prices.

In all these earlier models, if you wanted to start a new company or bring a new product to market, convincing the retailer to take your product was a huge barrier. An expensive sales team was essential. The retailer held the negotiating power as many products negotiated for a limited amount of shelf space. Wal-Mart designed its business model around this leverage, squeezing a relatively small number of suppliers to deliver ever-lower prices. In the centralized Wal-Mart era, going to Bentonville, Arkansas, to kowtow before the retail king was necessary for a product to get to market successfully.

Welcome to the new sales universe

Enter Amazon. The online giant, like the Internet itself, took a decentralized approach. It fostered not just evolution but a revolution in retail sales.

Where Wal-Mart has limited shelf space, Amazon's digital catalog can offer a nearly infinite variety of products. Where Wal-Mart achieves lower prices through negotiation and scale, Amazon achieves it through competition within its marketplace. For any given product, Wal-Mart limits and monitors selection and quality through in-house buyers, while Amazon welcomes many sellers and product versions but then adjusts the search position of those offerings based on conversion metrics, satisfaction metrics, and customer reviews. With Wal-Mart, everything is a negotiation, terms vary wildly, and larger competitors have a huge leg up on smaller ones. Amazon provides a much more level playing field for large and small companies alike. Where Wal-Mart is a retailer, Amazon is a collection of separate platforms for selling, warehousing, fulfillment, advertising, etc. — each of which has its own pricing and the ability to be used independently.

The death of geography

International readers may view this characterization of the change in retailing as Amazon-centric and/or U.S.-centric. There's little question that Amazon is driving the sea-change in the United States. But the rest of the globe, including online retailers like Alibaba, are following Amazon's lead. Amazon offers the same marketplace services in a growing list of countries (currently the U.S., Canada, Mexico, the U.K., Germany, France, Spain, Italy, Japan, China, and India, with many more to come). And if there aren't already more Chinese sellers online than U.S. sellers, there soon will be. Geography no longer matters much. That's a key part of the change.

Jeff Bezos' vision

Amazon started by leveraging the Internet to offer the "long tail" of millions of books, not just the small set of best sellers and curated books a physical store could offer. He leveraged this success to create the "everything store" where selection, competition, and fulfillment automation is the means to deliver any product at the best possible price.

Your new reach

This system that Amazon has built enables you to bring your products directly to customers. You set the price, you determine the marketing content, you support the customers. You get fast feedback. Are customers clicking? Buying? Returning? Writing reviews? You can learn and iterate quickly.

In short, Amazon has enabled small companies to focus on their core competencies around the product, and to outsource sales and logistics to reach customers around the world.

The bad news

Market entry barriers are low to non-existent, so you're competing on an open and mostly level playing field with the whole world — including the world's biggest and best, and those with the deepest pockets. Special supplier relationships, contracts, and the waning power of customer loyalty mean little. Anyone could replace your company and products tomorrow in this Wild West of selling.

> ## More than 2 million sellers
> have accounts on Amazon. Sure, not all are active, and many aren't private label sellers, but there are still probably tens of thousands of private label sellers in the U.S.[1]

As a result, competition is fiercer than ever, even for established businesses. In fact, it's the established companies that perhaps face the

---

[1] Perez, Sarah. "Amazon's Third-Party Sellers Ship…" *Tech Crunch*, Jan. 5, 2015, http://techcrunch.com/2015/01/05/amazon-third-party-sellers-2014/

highest risk of being left behind if they don't recognize how the playing field has changed.

And while Amazon provides a set of baseline services and the raw data to begin learning, it's not enough to be a top seller. Additional automation is needed to analyze that raw data, make it actionable, and close the gaps in communication with customers that Amazon doesn't fill.

Many of the top Amazon sellers have developed their own software to automate all this and ensure fast response times. A few of them have made their software available to other sellers. Our Efficient Era service (http://efficientera.com/) is one of those.

How this guide can help you

This guide is not for beginners. It is primarily for established manufacturers and private-label sellers who may have a year or two of online retailing experience but who want to move beyond manual management and grow. The basics for selling on Amazon are readily available elsewhere, including on Amazon's extensive "Selling on Amazon" Help pages and tutorials. (If you haven't already, you could do worse than reading every word there.)

Many of the existing resources out there, however, are for Amazon resellers or private-label beginners. An awful lot of books, webinars, podcasts, and consultants focus on finding new keywords, the latest tricks for rising in search results, listing optimization, etc. While these tactics have value, they may be missing the forest for the trees — particularly since Amazon frequently changes the algorithms and the conditions under which you're competing.

This guide is for more experienced sellers who recognize that there are no tricks or schemes, only winning strategies, best practices, and tools for leveraging data and closing the feedback loops that drive successful e-commerce. The strategies and insights laid out in these pages are based on hard-won experience from highly successful and long-term Amazon sellers. The tools mentioned in these pages, including the Efficient Era tools created by the author, automate the essential processes for success. The guide and these tools together will give you ideas for where to break new ground while laying out the baseline of best practices that will enable you to compete with the best in the world.

Skip around if you like. Mastering e-commerce requires a matrix of strategies, and it's not easy to talk about it in strictly linear form. As your experience grows, the information here will take on deeper meaning each time you revisit it.

The good news
Stiff competition is the downside of this new Amazoniverse. The upside? You have a much larger potential market!

Shoppers in 185 countries:
Amazon sellers in more than 100 countries served customers in 185 countries in 2015.[2]

No matter where you're reading this from, you can soon have customers on the other side of the world. And if you can do a good job of serving those customers, you can clean up. That's partly why participation in online marketplaces, whether as a reseller or a manufacturer with a private label, has become this decade's "get rich quick" scheme. There are dozens of resources available to help literally anyone, from brick-and-mortar retailers to retirees and recent graduates who can't otherwise find a job.

If your product is completely unique, you have a lot of options for selling it. E-commerce then becomes mostly about educating the right shoppers that it exists for them.

---

[2] Rao, Leena. "This Lesser-Known Amazon Business Is Growing Fast." *Fortune*, Jan. 5, 2016, http://fortune.com/2016/01/05/amazon-sellers-holidays/

But few products are truly that unique. Apples do compete with oranges if the shopper just wants a snack. Even products that appear unique usually have functional alternatives — and there are plenty of people ready to point out those alternatives.

The keys: Listen closely, react quickly

This means that most of us have to be very competitive, listening closely and responding quickly to the action. The margin for errors is slim. We can't afford to be off our game in any way or, simply put, we'll be beat.

This new retailing world demands new approaches. Specifically, it's characterized by four essential traits:

- Ever-increasing speed.
- Enough data to choke on.
- A flywheel effect in which sales beget more sales.
- Powerful feedback loops to learn from.

Each of these traits requires you to effectively manage your business. Here's how:

1. Get ready to move like lightning.

The first trait is simply a facet of the increasing pace of life, driven by technology. This acceleration affects retailing by raising customer expectations, including the expectation that things should happen in seconds, minutes, or hours, not days or weeks. (One example is the growing interest in one-hour delivery service.) Our increasing use of technology also can affect sales velocity and repercussions. For instance, online promotions that work better than expected, perhaps because of an unexpected social media share, can inadvertently lay waste to inventory (and margins) in 30 minutes.

These conditions require unprecedented business agility. Speedy recognition and responses — to customers and market events and conditions — are critical to survival. Amazon in particular is a fast-moving machine, and as a third-party seller, you're working in the midst of the pistons and gears. You'll see peers and competitors who make missteps, lose fingers, or get pulled in and ground to a pulp. To survive, you have to be alert, informed, and nimble.

Fortunately, this guide can help.

2. Surf the data tsunami.

Never before have sellers had so much rich data to help them manage customer relationships and make decisions. Meanwhile, customers also have more data for decisions. Think in terms of the classic Plan, Do, Check, Act (PDCA) or Deming Cycle, a staple of nearly a half-century of management theory and process or product improvement efforts. (See http://en.wikipedia.org/wiki/PDCA.)

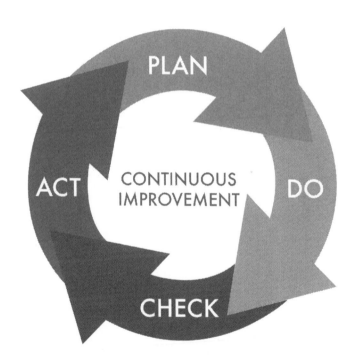

Every time you make a product available online, every time a customer clicks your product page or hits "Complete order," that action kicks off a stream of data that both you and shoppers can use. Amazon certainly monitors that data and uses it to make changes — from a product's search results placement to which seller wins the buy box. That way, over time, Amazon maximizes the benefits of every transaction. You can, too.

But the available data can be overwhelming. Focusing on the wrong things or spending too many resources to interpret it can be as deadly as ignoring the insights completely. The tools available to help are indispensable — one of the best investments you'll make. You simply can't expect long-term success without them.

Tool Description: Sales Charts with Annotations

Efficient Era's "contextual event" system and time-series charts are vital for being able to process the flood of data — without this system, you can easily find yourself drowning instead of surfing. By default, our sales charts will show you historical sales charts for all your products. But Efficient Era also makes that data uniquely actionable by showing key events in the timeline and letting you add custom events and track how your sales were affected by them. Directly track what's impacting your performance — whether a recently launched coupon campaign or a holiday event — with Efficient Era's contextual sales charts.

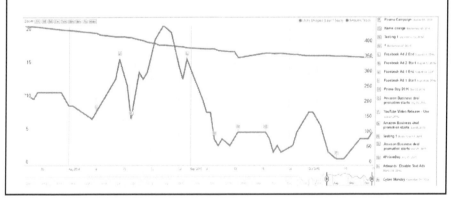

---

3. Understand and capitalize on the flywheel effect.

An even more significant trait of the new sales model is its iterative nature — often characterized as the flywheel effect. In short, the search algorithms that drive online marketplaces ensure that the more successful your selling, the more you can sell.

Definition: The flywheel effect

"The flywheel effect" is a shorthand term for a vicious (or virtuous) cycle — what you get when the better a product sells, the easier it is to sell more. Or vice versa. Another parallel is inertia and the first law of thermodynamics: A product in motion tends to stay in motion, and a product at rest tends to stay at rest. The trick is to inject energy into the flywheel, by almost any means necessary, to get it moving. Then it becomes a whole lot easier to keep it moving or accelerate it.

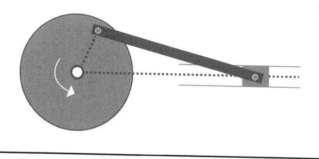

Unfortunately, the reverse is true, too. The day your product launches into an online marketplace, it becomes a needle at the bottom of a very big haystack. It'll remain there, invisible, until you begin driving traffic to the product detail page, making sales, and earning positive customer reviews. Then the flywheel begins to creak into action, sifting your needle slowly up toward the surface. It takes significant time and effort to overcome that "cold start" to improve shoppers' ability to find your product, and mistakes can bring the flywheel to a dead halt again. But once it's moving well, it becomes a beneficial cycle that, when well managed, can hum along with relatively little tending.

So how do you nudge the flywheel into action?

4. Encourage and close feedback loops, including customer opinions after sales.

The flywheel is driven by several things, most importantly historical conversion rates, sales, and customer opinions. Customers and the customer voice have always been important, but never more so than now.

Some analysts have noted, "As with any business, reviews can make or break you." That's grossly understated. In e-commerce, good reviews are *much more* important than with "any" business. Take a restaurant in a tourist corridor, for example. The locals might swap reviews and, if the food is so-so, they'll know not to go there (and have a better sense of the alternatives). Despite the growth of services such as Yelp and TripAdvisor, however, a lot of people passing through either don't know any better or will sacrifice quality for convenience.

E-commerce customers have no similar blinders. Every former customer's review might as well be painted in neon on the side of your building. Online marketplaces put you closer to customers, but that means you're closer to unhappy customers, too. And the prominence of reviews and power of social networking give them more influence over buying decisions than ever.

So it's crucial to manage opinions and communication as much as possible. The way to do that is to treat every interaction as part of a loop that can be closed to benefit everyone.

Definition: Feedback loops
A feedback loop, for our purposes, is a cycle in which the output of a process — such as a customer purchase — is used as an input into the same process. Asking new buyers for product reviews that encourage a purchase by other buyers is one example. Others include feeding complaints data into product development and incorporating customer insights about a product's uses into that product's marketing. Feedback loops turn otherwise linear, "one and done" exchanges — purchase, shipment, receipt, the end —

---

into ongoing cycles of interaction. These relationships power the sales flywheel.

Enough talking already? Let's move on to actions.

Efficient Era

Chapter 1 —
Four Winning Strategies for Success

In this brave new Amazon sales era, those who are successful usually follow four strategies (whether consciously or intuitively).

1. Identify a coherent set of multiple products you can provide better than anyone else.

One great product isn't enough. Too many things can go wrong, and you have too little control over marketplace changes or competitors. The flywheel will crush anyone who stakes everything on one product. To capitalize on repeat business, market familiarity, and your own growing expertise, identify a family, series, or collection of goods that will fill customer needs and build on your company's strengths. If you're already producing a few winners, great! Start there.

Depending on what you're good at, you might leverage:

- A technical expertise: Identify a set of related products that rely on that skill set.
- Market or demographic insight: Cater to a specific audience (such as scrapbookers or robotics competitors) with a variety of products that speak to that audience.

- Logistics: Capitalize on your network and systems to sell unusually large, heavy, or awkwardly shaped products, for instance.
- Foresight: Be faster and smarter than anyone else about identifying new or underserved market niches with products tailored to each.

Whatever your approach to identifying and grouping your products, look at them in light of the competition. In the e-commerce world, you have almost perfect visibility into your competitors' products — as they do into yours. That's not all bad. Use that visibility to gain insight and make decisions based on the five factors that influence any product's success:

Market size. You can get a rough idea of the size of any market and the sales of any competitor before deciding whether or how to launch your product. One way is by tracking daily changes in a top seller's inventory level. (See one method for this at http://provenprofitsacademy.com/how-to-estimate-your-amazon-sales-before-you-buy.) Another way is to look at seller rating and product review quantities. Amazon says that 10 to 20 percent of buyers leave seller feedback, while others estimate that fewer than 5 percent of buyers leave product reviews[3]. Multiply those estimates by the numbers of ratings. (Realize that this percentage may or may not be particularly accurate for every product category.) Either way, you can extrapolate a rough sense of weekly sales, and thus the overall market, and make appropriate decisions in light of your assessment of the competition's strengths and your own.

Features. Every product has an online listing, and between the listing details and features mentioned in reviews, it's easy to get a sense of which features most matter to various types of customers or for different applications, which command a price premium, and which might make your product stand out.

---

[3] Amazon, "Why Don't I Have More Feedback?" Feedback FAQs, http://tinyurl.com/hkw3n8w, plus Efficient Era data

Quality. Through Amazon's product reviews, you have visibility into thousands of customer experiences with products like yours or that yours can replace. To give yourself a huge advantage, track and study this information. Mine the gems in the frustrations, delights, and ideas customers describe, and use the insight to solve the problems and improve your own products.

Price. Every change in a competitor's price can be followed. Before you even decide if you can offer a competitive product, you can and should track your competitors' pricing and model the pricing for your own. There are plenty of price tracking tools to help you readily know what competitors are doing.

A lot of the advice buzzing through the e-commerce world focuses on winning the buy box by setting the lowest prices, down to the penny. But part of the reason you're a private label seller may be to avoid the pitfalls of commodity pricing. That doesn't mean that private label products aren't also highly competitive. Do your research. One strategy is to focus on segments with reasonably stable prices based on cost structures, rather than the more volatile product categories. In that case, you could use a cost-plus pricing model.

Another strategy that works for more niche-oriented products is a fixed margin or contribution margin model. Similarly, products whose sales respond well to promotions — that is, items that most everyone needs and that people buy repeatedly, such as batteries, chargers, or socks — may be successful with a higher list price but frequent discounts or sales that effect a "pumping" action on sales.

The promise and peril of loss leaders

Brick and mortar businesses have a case for loss-leader pricing models. Similarly, Amazon's loss leading strategy appears to be paying off, because every sale on the site generates revenue for them — but the same is not often true for individual sellers. There's nothing to prevent shoppers from buying your loss leader and then switching to competitors for everything else, and unlike Amazon, you probably can't survive for a couple of decades on almost no

---

profit. Some sellers will successfully take a loss on products for as long as a year to deter competitors, and others use a low-cost product variation to entice shoppers to buy a more profitable variation. These strategies can be successful, but should be used with caution and careful attention to data.

Regardless of how well you optimize all other factors, if you don't have a good product at the right price, your efforts aren't going to pay off. The speed and level of competition in online marketplaces has a magnifying effect on mistakes. To prevent such mistakes, before you launch any product:

- Figure out the market price for that product.
- Determine your costs at the quantities in which you can get it made.
- Do a miniature business model calculation, including Amazon fulfillment costs and shipping, to see if you can compete with a profit margin healthy enough for you to survive. If the answer is no, look for another product.

Time to market. The final factor that influences product success is speed. If you want newly developed products to be leaders, you've got to move fast. Be sure to factor sourcing or manufacturing time, shipping time, and marketplace listing time into your assessment of whether you can feasibly be the first to market. Or perhaps there are other considerations that might make a strong second okay. Track your competitors' product pages — they'll be tracking yours. You can watch their product launches, often before sales take off. And when you're the one launching, be prepared: The advantages of getting to market first are huge, but the time until competitors follow is short. Capitalize while you can.

2. For everything else you offer, replicate the quality and service of the best in the world.

In other words, be as good as everyone else on the bulk of your catalog, *plus* specialize in the area you identified above — where an expertise, technological edge, service capability, or market insight allows you to be outstanding.

3. Proactively manage your marketplace presence to appropriately close feedback loops.

It's not sufficient simply to automate a feed from your online store, no matter how successful, to an online marketplace such as Amazon. You wouldn't open a retail location and walk away, would you? Doing the equivalent in e-commerce can quickly result in disarrayed product pages, undercut prices, customer questions that languish unanswered, negative reviews, or competition from pirate sellers with counterfeit products, among other hazards. More importantly, automation simply does not take advantage of the platform's specific, and frequently changing, opportunities.

Orient the entire business (including marketing, sales, service, product management, and product development) toward using the available information to close the feedback loops that drive sales. That includes feedback from:

- Individual customers, who should influence your product development or sourcing and who can help, or hinder, your sales efforts.
- The marketplace owner (e.g., Amazon), which sets (and may change) the rules you must follow for everything from how you display your product in photos to how you can promote it. The marketplace also provides feedback in the form of sales velocities, advertising efficiency, inventory status, and a plethora of other useful information.
- The market as a whole, including competitive information, about your product success.

Closing these feedback loops is critical to everything from offering your product at the right price to building rewarding customer relationships.

Really good sellers double down on these sources of feedback and make sure they're really good at obtaining all available information and responding as described in the rest of this guide.

4. Take advantage of helpful tools and advice.

The speed of online markets makes it necessary to have tools that can monitor and analyze the data flying at you and either respond automatically to close a feedback loop or alert you for a decision before you're overwhelmed. This is true, to a greater or lesser degree, for all online marketplaces, from eBay to Alibaba. We'll focus on Amazon because it sets the trends.

The Plugable story

Plugable Technologies was started in September of 2009 with a goal of "building a better device company." I had worked for 15 years as a software developer at other companies, and I saw an opportunity to deliver plug-and-play products while hitting a higher quality bar and having better support to back them up. I hoped the extra cost of doing things that way would work out by focusing on channels where product reviews matter, like Amazon.

The first 1.5 years was just me, no employees, with my days filled by completing forms, setting up our website, negotiating with vendors, listing products, and supporting customers. I was excited to build a physical company with a no-warehouse model by leveraging FBA. I wanted to focus on technology and customer support and not have to worry about selling and the logistics of individual customer orders. For big shipments, I would rent a U-Haul truck, drive to the customs bonded warehouse to take delivery out of the container, and use the U-Haul as a temporary warehouse for a few hours. I would crawl inside, shuffle boxes, label them all for shipment to Amazon, and then drive them to UPS for same-day turnaround. Then I'd return my "warehouse" to U-Haul.

Having to do all the work myself motivated me to automate as much as possible. I didn't want to keep checking for new product reviews, so I created Python scripts to email me when new feedback

---

was posted. Same with post-order emails, notification of seller feedback, downloading reports for further analysis, and more. That paid off.

For a long time I debated whether to offer this automation to others or keep it as a competitive advantage. After a few years, it became clear that keeping the software ahead of other alternatives required full-time developers, so we decided to give up this potential advantage and offer it to others to share the cost of development. We've recently made all these tools available at efficientera.com and dozens of other sellers are taking advantage of them. They can speed and automate the best practices discussed in this guide so your business can become more successful and you can more easily manage growth.

—Bernie Thompson, Founder, Plugable Technologies

Amazon has a lot of built-in tools and APIs available to help you capture data and make it actionable. But a few important tools are missing:

- Amazon has a system for sending emails between sellers and customers (through their servers, so they can monitor what's passing), but they don't have any *automatic* way for sellers to communicate with buyers. Wouldn't it be helpful to send an email with extra product information when a product ships, or to send a request for a product review about the time you know the product has arrived?
- Sellers can use an Amazon API to be notified of negative seller feedback. But surprisingly, if you'd like to thank customers who leave positive seller feedback — and prompt them for a product review, too — there's no way to be notified of the positive ones and automate any response.
- Amazon also doesn't provide any automated way to alert sellers or brand owners to a new product review, whether negative or positive. In fact, an API for such notification was removed in late 2010, probably because Amazon didn't want to

make it quite so easy for sellers to copy valuable reviews outside of the Amazon site. And even if you notice a review, there is no program available to sellers that provides the customer's contact information. That makes it hard to treat negative feedback as a customer service incident, and therefore harder to fix anything for that customer.

- Amazon provides lots of charting and reports, with a tendency to focus on aggregate sales because that's what matters to them. But as a brand owner, you need to analyze sales of individual products — what's succeeding, what's not, and why.
- Amazon takes actions for and against your products — actions like switching categories, taking away the buy box, or suspending listings. Sometimes they notify you, and sometimes they don't. But it's important to your success to know immediately, every time.
- A lot of functionality available via Amazon APIs is underused or not used at all by smaller sellers, in part because of the complexity and intimidation factor.

External tools like those available from Efficient Era (http://efficientera.com/) fill all these gaps and more.

Got a product now?
Good. We'll explore the key ways to make it a success: closing the feedback loops that will swarm around it.

But first, let's address a few oddities of the Amazon online marketplace — the beast at whose mercy you'll be putting your business. You need to know it inside and out.

Chapter 2 — In the Belly of the Beast: Understanding Amazon

When you become a seller on the Amazon marketplace, it's wise to know everything you can about what you're getting into — what's there that can hurt you, and what's there to help.

1. Sling the lingo.

Understanding your options can be a challenge complicated both by the slang of the Amazoniverse and by program names that strive to be intuitive but often overlap: AmazonBasics, Amazon Prime, Amazon Warehouse Deals, Fulfillment By Amazon, Seller Central, Vendor Central, Vendor Express. The glossary of Amazon terms and programs at the end of this guide may help.

2. Choose the right relationship.

Amazon offers two competing ways to sell products through its marketplace: wholesale (a.k.a. Amazon retail) or direct-to-consumer (a.k.a. the Amazon Marketplace).

Be wary of Amazon retail.

With a wholesale relationship, you sell your product to Amazon, and they handle everything after that. This is closer to the Wal-Mart model. The margins and fees Amazon expects vary significantly, depending on the relationship you negotiate. You don't control consumer pricing, inventory, or other critical factors for success. In this case, you work with the retail group, are considered a vendor, and interact with Amazon through the Vendor Central website, although if you're just getting started, you'll probably be using the Vendor Express program.

To date, most private-label sellers have found this relationship unsuccessful, unless their product is completely without competition. Amazon's pricing algorithms don't care about the success of your particular product (vs. the same product from your competitors); they're focused more on their own total revenue and price competition with other marketplaces. That programmatic, yet lackadaisical, pricing approach can price your product out of the market.

In addition, Amazon's inventory stocking algorithms don't have the knowledge, instincts, or tolerance for risk you can apply. As a result, there have been notable examples of products that became very successful on the Marketplace, but then were brought over to Retail, which caused a large drop in sales because of poor pricing and out-of-stock events beyond the seller's (vendor's) control.

Finally, once you've sold a product through Amazon retail, you can't go back to the Amazon Marketplace and change any product characteristics. Most of them will be fixed permanently by Amazon retail. Someday retail may improve its offering, and this book can still be useful for someone who chooses this way to work with Amazon, but the advice here is primarily targeted at the other alternative: the Marketplace.

Look first to Amazon Marketplace.
With the direct method represented by the Marketplace, you sell products directly to consumers using Amazon's platform and its services for listing products, taking orders, fulfillment, etc. The fees, which are fixed for large and small sellers, are communicated transparently. You control pricing, inventory levels, communication with customers (for the most part), and the details of how your product is presented. You work with Amazon's Marketplace group, are considered a seller, and interact with Amazon through the Seller Central website. All this control over your own success means you have a lot of responsibility and work. But it's possible manage things

simply at first, to get started, while optimizing your strategies, tools, and processes over time. This guide can help.

3. Don't ignore the fine print.

Regardless of how you sell on Amazon, pay close attention to prohibited activities. (Find them at http://tinyurl.com/9svozy6.) They have millions of sellers and products to police, and it's Amazon's sandbox; they set the rules. Amazon is generally happy to have you — they make more profit on third-party sales than on most of their own branded products — but you're able to play by their consent, which can be and sometimes is withdrawn[4].

> # 80-90% of products
> sold through Amazon in many categories are from third-party sellers.[5]

If something goes wrong, your Amazon business, which may become extremely valuable, could be taken away. Factor that risk into your decision making. Further, avoid account suspensions, listing suspensions, or other difficulties caused by breaking rules — from major offenses such as product counterfeiting or not gaining approval before entering restricted categories to less obvious errors such as using a .com business name as your seller name (which breaks the rule about not directing traffic outside of Amazon, even if inadvertently). Amazon often won't say why an account is suspended — just that it is. The better you know the rules, the less likely you'll ever need to wonder.

---

[4] "Amazon.com: Third-Party Sellers Drive Profitability," *Seeking Alpha*, April 1, 2016, http://seekingalpha.com/article/3962561-amazon-com-third-party-sellers-drive-profitability. Also Greg Bensinger, "Amazon's Third-Party Merchants Are a Growing Piece of the Sales Pie," *Wall Street Journal*, Jan. 5, 2015, http://blogs.wsj.com/digits/2015/01/05/amazons-third-party-merchants-a-growing-piece-of-the-sales-pie/
[5] R.W. Baird data in "Amazon.com: Third-Party Sellers Drive Profitability," *Seeking Alpha*, April 1, 2016, http://seekingalpha.com/article/3962561-amazon-com-third-party-sellers-drive-profitability.

> # Broken rules
> are responsible for a majority of suspensions, according to consultants who help get accounts reinstated when misunderstandings take place. Those same consultants note that it's not easy to get a second chance.[6]

Working successfully with Amazon depends in part on solid relationships with Seller Support staff. Don't start off on the wrong foot.

That said, the Amazon guidelines do include grey areas, and most highly successful sellers push those boundaries a bit by, for instance, making it easier for customers to leave product feedback. One of the more important reasons for reading the terms of service is to truly understand Amazon's perspective and the spirit, not merely the letter, of the rules.

> **Tip: Remember the customer.**
> You can push the grey areas when it benefits all parties if you do it while respecting Amazon's ultimate goals: happy, returning customers. Recognize and honor the principles of customer satisfaction that drive most Amazon rules.

4. Take advantage of the Professional selling plan level.

Amazon offers both an Individual and a Professional selling plan in the United States; the Individual level is known as Basic in the United Kingdom. The plans offer different fee structures and benefits; anyone reading this guide wants the Professional level and will be commonly referred to as a Professional Seller. There's a monthly fee, but unless

---

[6] "Is It Amazon Account Suspension Season?", Sellerengine.com, http://sellerengine.com/amazon-account-suspension-season/, and "Avoid Being Suspended by Amazon," ChannelAdvisor, http://ssc.channeladvisor.com/avoid-being-suspending-amazon, and Malik, Jordan, "Why Amazon Sellers Are Banned...", http://jordanmalik.com/blog/why-amazon-sellers-are-banned-and-what-theyre-not-banned-for/

you only have one or two products, you can't expect to get sufficient data for good decisions or manage your account and inventory entirely through their online management interface.

While we're at it, yes, Amazon does have higher selling levels than "Professional". This used to be called Platinum seller status.[7] Rumors fly about this invitation-only program for large sellers with solid track records and outstanding sales and customer service metrics — in other words, those who make money for themselves and for Amazon. As with most else on Amazon, the flywheel metaphor applies here, too: The better you do, the better you can do. Sellers fortunate enough to be invited obtain a potential variety of benefits, including account managers, technical support, more frequent settlement payments, and participation in beta programs.

Make that invitation, and the success it implies, one of your goals.

5. Take advantage of the Brand Registry program.

Join the Brand Registry program, whose benefits are enormously significant for controlling your product listings and simplifying your inventory management. Only a few product categories are ineligible.

At one time, Amazon's basic assumption was that manufacturers were never sellers, too. As a result, for any given ASIN, the system drew what it considered the best titles, photos, product feature text, and descriptions, from the contributions of multiple (re)sellers. This could be chaotic, so Amazon would start locking down the listings from further changes as sales grew. This process was known as ASIN hardening, and the idea was to offer shoppers the best information about a given product — that is, the information Amazon deemed most likely to lead to a sale —as drawn from all possible sources.

But this model assumes third-party sellers are offering an identical (probably branded) product, not value-added private label products. And that product descriptions and marketing shouldn't need to change

---

[7] "What Is Amazon Platinum Seller Status?", SellerEngine, http://sellerengine.com/what-is-amazon-platinum-seller-status/

or evolve. For professional private-label sellers, really describing your product accurately, with the latest information and in terms that best attract buyers, is key to success. You need control of your listing to the degree possible. For products that need work with other products, it becomes an absolute necessity to update your listing with the latest compatibility information so customers can successfully buy a compatible product (and don't ding you with a negative review for getting it wrong). You also need some defense against counterfeiters trying to pass off inferior products from *your* product page and platform.

The Brand Registry identifies you as the authority on your brand. Head off trouble, including listing hijacking, by applying from the start. You don't have to have a UPC or EAN for each product, but you will need a similarly unique and immutable identifying attribute such as a model number, catalog number, or manufacturer's part number, for instance. This unique number should be included in your product listing, if it isn't already. Amazon will use it to assign the product a permanent 16-character Global Catalog Identification (GCID) number, which is distinct from the product listing's ASIN, which can change.

Brand Registry participation isn't a panacea. It gives you certain authority to create and maintain the product detail page, but you still may find your listing hijacked, with real or counterfeit products being sold by unauthorized resellers or have trouble making specification updates because Amazon's retail group contributions will still trump yours. But it helps significantly.

6. Understand your fulfillment options and Amazon Prime eligibility.

Amazon is a unique online marketplace in that it will handle fulfillment for you. Fulfillment by Amazon (FBA) — as distinct from fulfillment by merchant or FBM — gives you a leg up in the competition for the buy box. Perhaps more important, FBA is the primary way to make your products eligible for Amazon Prime status, which you want. There's little question that a product with the Prime flag will both receive better search placement and sell more.

2.4 times more sales:
Amazon Prime members spend more than twice as much annually, on average, as other Amazon customers: $1,200 a year vs. $500.[8]

Recently, Amazon has expanded the Prime program to include a category called Seller Fulfilled Prime, in which sellers with metrics over certain thresholds can use the Prime-eligible flag on select FBM products when they can guarantee shipment to meet the Prime guarantee.[9] This program is regional and based on the shopper's default shipping address, so sellers can participate regionally even if they can't manage the costs of two-day shipping to the entire United States.

Amazon FBA is very price competitive for all but the smallest and largest products. It lets you grow your business without building a pick and pack operation with many employees. And it has only a few downsides: Amazon expects you to turn your inventory every 6 to 12 months and will charge you more if you can't, Amazon also has high standards for FBA, will suspend your product for many reasons including high return rates (even if it's not a faulty product!), and FBA walks you into a whole bunch of potential tax complexity with several countries in Europe and every US state with an Amazon warehouse.

See the inventory management section for more about the choice between FBA and FBM.

Tip: Know how hazmat classifications affect your fulfillment choice.

---

[8] Gustafson, Krystina. "Amazon Just Had Its Biggest Sales Day Ever," CNBC, July 13, 2016, http://www.cnbc.com/2016/07/13/amazon-prime-day-is-biggest-day-for-online-retailer-ever.html

[9] Enright, Allison. "Amazon Lets Sellers Handle Some Prime Fulfillment, and It's Paying Off," *Internet Retailer*, Jan. 6, 2016, http://www.internetretailer.com/2016/01/06/how-amazon-seller-fulfilled-prime-works

Some products or product ingredients may be considered hazardous materials for shipping purposes. (See http://tinyurl.com/hog39hh.) The list of possible hazmat is long and encompasses everything from antibacterial products and the alcohol in vanilla extract to stove fuels and lithium batteries. Unfortunately, you may not be able to use FBA for these products, though there are exceptions by invitation only. A hazardous material also can affect the information or documentation you need to provide when creating your product listing, inventory shipments, or both.

Amazon relies primarily on the guidance of authorities such as the U.S. Department of Transportation and U.S. Postal Service for identifying hazardous materials. (See the former at http://www.phmsa.dot.gov/regulations.) You can also get questions answered by contacting the Hazardous Materials Information Center at 1-800-HMR-4922 or http://www.phmsa.dot.gov/hazmat/standards-rulemaking/hmic. In other jurisdictions, check with the International Air Transport Association (IATA) and national authorities about "dangerous goods." Even if your product doesn't qualify, it may still be subject to a hazmat review, in which case you'll need to submit additional documentation about your product prior to listing it. See the troubleshooting chapter for more information.

7. Be prepared to go beyond your Seller Central dashboard.

One advantage of the Amazon marketplace is the rich data the company makes available to you. The Seller Central dashboard provides plenty to start with, and you particularly need to stay on top of notifications there, but recognize that the dashboard really is only a start. It's generally not your most efficient way to manage numerous products, access the data over time, or turn that information into decisions. For starters, it provides only a snapshot, and very little in the way of historical tracking. To obtain trend information, you'll have to download data over time and assemble and correlate it yourself. Of course, the huge flat files, from product listings to inventory spreadsheets, that pass between sellers and Amazon over time can be unwieldy and difficult to interpret or work with, too.

As already noted, if you're not an Excel geek or closet software engineer, there are many resources available, including consultants who will do this for you or tools that can help you do it yourself.

8. Be aware of, but wary of, Amazon financing.

A few years back, Amazon introduced a lending program intended to help sellers grow. Since the company arguably knows more about your business than you do, there's no application or qualification process. It simply offers a loan amount, which can be considerable, at reasonable interest rates and fixed, often relatively short terms. It's all too easy, frankly — which can bite sellers who come to rely on that capital to operate, only to suddenly find that once the first loan is paid off, the offer may not be renewed.

So treat such credit sources as a viable option, particularly for holiday inventory bubbles and other short-term needs, but one that you may not have again later.

9. Understand Amazon categories.

People often use the word "categories" to refer to different things, and even Amazon support pages throw the word around loosely. In addition, there are differences in the browse nodes and hierarchies between Amazon.com and international Amazon marketplaces. Finally, Amazon often adds, refines, or removes categories without notice. Even Amazon staff sometimes get confused. But the browse nodes are important because each comes with inherent keywords that people use to search and buy. Here is a primer:

Get the terminology straight. The category your product is assigned has two major parts: an assigned department and one or more, potentially several, assigned browse nodes.

Departments are fundamental. Every product is assigned to a single, top-level department (e.g. Consumer Electronics, Beauty, Automotive, etc.). This is what most people mean when they talk of a product's "category." These departments match what's visible to muggles on the Amazon.com site.

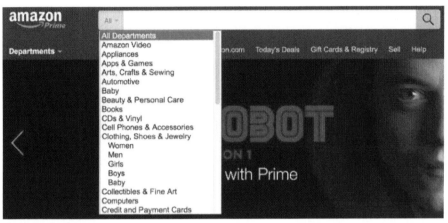

Amazon's departments

For geeks, these departments also match one-to-one with the "ProductData" element in Amazon's XML API, which then defines sub-schemas of XML for different product characteristics, depending on which department is chosen.

Amazon's mindset is that each department may be treated quite differently in terms of the information shown for each product, the search rules that apply, and so on. And each department is managed by different teams within Amazon. There are currently 27 departments your product can be assigned to, and getting the wrong one could significantly hurt you.

Each department may have its own "inventory loader" spreadsheet, which asks for different data about the products. When listing new products, if you're using the spreadsheet method of uploading product data, *you'll effectively be selecting your product's category by which spreadsheet you choose.*

Browse nodes may be complicated. Next, within each department assignment, every product has one or more assigned "browse nodes." Browse nodes are a detailed tree of sub-categories, with a top-level, "root" browse node whose name may be similar to the department name. Third-party sellers are now limited to just one top-level browse node — one root node — per product, such as Electronics or Clothing, Shoes, and Jewelry.

The possible browse nodes are defined by department-specific browse tree guides (BTGs) that break the department into hundreds or thousands of subcategories.[10] These subcategories each have an associated structure and a number, and sometimes an Item Type Keyword text field. When listing your product in the U.S., you can assign a single subcategory, and two may be assigned in some other geographies. But Amazon can support many browse node assignments per ASIN.

When using some ways of listing new products (through the Seller Central interface, for instance), you may not be asked for your product's department. Rather, you'll assign a specific browse node, and the department that contains that browse node will automatically be assigned. (In other words, if you assign a heated car seat cover to the Custom Fit Seat Covers browse node, the product will automatically be put in the Automotive department.)

What's in a browse node? Each browse node comes with an identifying Node ID number, and every root node has a number of — sometimes many — dependent nodes. Node IDs may have a varying number of characters, and the IDs in any given root node typically end with, rather than beginning with, the same number. For instance, node IDs 2795108031 and 64348031 are both in the Beauty and Personal Care root node.

---

[10] Amazon: http://tinyurl.com/z7cshlx

Departments, categories, and nodes at a glance
Department: Defines which Browse Tree Guide to use. Often called a category.
Root node: The top-level browse node in a tree, with a name that is often similar to the department name.
Parent node: Any node (root or otherwise) with dependent "leaf" nodes.
Leaf node: The end point of a node browse path, with no dependents.
Category: A fuzzy term that may be used to reference any or all of the above.
Subcategory: A similarly fuzzy term that is more likely to be used for a leaf node or a parent node that is not a root node.

Any nodes that have their own dependents are called parent nodes; those without dependents are called leaf nodes (and represent the end of the line in a browse path). A specific parent or leaf node may be what people mean when they discuss a product's category or subcategory.

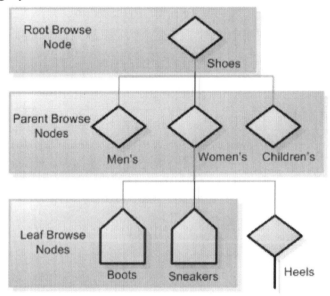

Source: Amazon AWS, http://tinyurl.com/h7hbmgd

The series of nodes in a chain is called a browse path, and it's this browse path that may appears in the "bread crumbs" during searches.

1-24 of 84 results for **Home & Kitchen : Kitchen & Dining : Cookware : "popcorn machine"**

Show results for

‹ Any Category
‹ Home & Kitchen
‹ Kitchen & Dining
Cookware
    Specialty Cookware (3)
+ See more

SPONSORED BY GREAT NORTHERN POPCORN COMPANY

Great Northern Popcorn Machines
› Shop now

Browse paths like this one — Home & Kitchen > Kitchen & Dining > Cookware — may be indicated both in "breadcrumbs" and the browse menu at left in search results screens. Note that there is at least one more child node in Cookware called "Specialty Cookware."

Leaf nodes are your friends. When assigning a product to a node, "drill down" to put your product in the most relevant, narrowest leaf node possible. All the parent nodes and the root node higher in the hierarchy — and their keywords — will automatically be associated.

Tip: Don't browse. Find instead.
The Seller Central panel for selecting a new product's "category" offers two choices: browsing or simply entering the product and clicking "Find category." Use the latter. "Find category" displays potential browse nodes and paths with the opportunity to drill down and refine your search, and drilling down displays a more comprehensive list of subcategories — category refinements — including many that don't appear at all in the browse choices.[11]

Once you've selected a leaf node for your product, perform a search on three or four of your most obvious keywords. On the results page, check which parent nodes appear in the browse navigation menus at the left of the screen. The top five will be most relevant categories for

---

[11] Bueno, Tina Marie. "How to Choose the Best Amazon Product Category," April 26, 2016, http://www.ilovetoreview.com/amazon-category/

the keyword you searched. Your product should be in one of those, preferable one that appears for all of your most obvious keywords.

Category relevance counts. Not long ago, savvy sellers submitted tickets to Seller Support asking to have their products added to multiple browse nodes, increasing the likelihood that the product might appear in a search… even if some of those categories were a stretch. This practice is now frowned on by Amazon, which is limiting third-party sellers to one category, even while putting its Amazon branded products in several. (See the section on competing with the house for more information.) It's become much harder to add categories even when they are relevant.

You don't want to be in categories that *aren't* relevant, anyhow. That's because the associated keywords can be harmful. If you're selling antique typewriter keys as a decorative item or jewelry supply, don't ask to be in Office Supplies on the theory that people interested in office supplies will be interested in related decor. If people click through to your page and then don't buy, your ratio of conversions to page views drops, and you'll lose search results ranking as a result. When the category's keywords don't result in good conversions, their *cumulative impact will be negative.*

What's important is to be in the right categories — the most relevant ones — and no others. If customers do use multiple categories to search and then buy, great. Try to get that product in those categories — but don't guess at others or assume more is necessarily better.

Recognize that some departments are gated.
Amazon requires sellers to request permission to participate in certain departments, such as beauty products, clothing, automotive products, and children's toys. In addition, re-selling certain known brands requires a one-time fee. These "brand gating" measures have developed because Amazon wants to be certain that customers will get first-rate products and service, without concerns about fakes, products that don't meet safety or regulatory standards, or goods that are simply illegal. If you make or sell products in the most controlled categories, there's a good chance you're already aware of the issues and will have

no trouble establishing your credentials and meeting the category requirements to sell on Amazon, too.

That said, category and brand restrictions, including entry fees, are on the increase as Amazon works with sellers to combat counterfeiting and focus on quality. The fees are unlikely to affect private-label sellers; it's a much better time to be a private-label seller than it is to be involved in retail arbitrage. But changes in this area will continue. Stay on top of them.

Download BTGs for your product.

The browse tree system is documented in the browse tree guides (BTGs) for each root node. The latest versions of these guides, in spreadsheet form, are available from Seller Central. Parent nodes are greyed out to force the selection of leaf nodes for that parent.

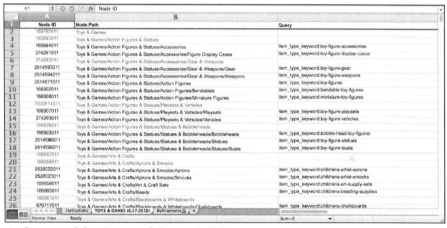

A glimpse of the Toys and Games BTG.

Identify the relevant node(s) for your product.

Sellers choose the appropriate browse node and path for their products, down to the lowest relevant leaf node (or nodes, since a product might be equally relevant to two or more). If you're using flat files to upload inventory information, you'll need to take note of the node name and ID.

One thing that is invisible to you, but critical for your success, is the set of Amazon search keywords associated with each browse node. Each node has associated keywords, and may also have negative keywords — those that identify what the product is not. For instance, if you sell car battery chargers or jump-starting devices, "auto" and "automotive" are likely to be associated keywords, and "phone" might be a negative keyword in your category. Shoppers searching for an iPhone charger are not looking to buy your trickle charger, and the negative keyword serves as a filter to keep the wrong products from showing (and from having their page view and conversion ratios suffer as a result).

These associated keywords are among the reasons that it's important to be in the right nodes and to stay away from the wrong ones. This is complicated by the fact that Amazon does not provide any list of either node keywords or negative keywords. You have to surmise and test for them in experimental searches.

In addition, if your product would make sense in several leaf nodes, put it where it has a shot of ranking at or near the top — that is, with the fewest competitors in that node. There's evidence that products near the top of their categories get a search results boost beyond what sheer sales numbers would warrant. So pick categories that are as narrow or niched as possible while still being fully relevant.

Keep tabs on your product's category over time.
Category mapping is a living entity that shifts. When a new type of product arises, it starts out in the browse node that seems most appropriate to the listing seller. If it starts selling well and everyone wants one, competitors join in, and Amazon may eventually create a new leaf node (subcategory) for that specific type of product.

Hoverboards provide an example. Originally listed in a generic consumer electronics browse node, the product was reassigned several times before eventually getting its own hoverboard leaf node. Later, when fires made product safety a concern, Amazon removed a bunch of listings, sales dropped, and eventually Amazon removed that leaf node for a while.

Less dramatic changes occur frequently and without notice, and products get shuffled around by Amazon as a result. This is especially true if you're working in areas of new technology —virtual reality headsets, say — or faddish consumer products. The decisions may be based on little understanding of the product — with over 480 million products listed, Amazon can't be familiar with them all. But your product's category can have a big effect on sales, and it also affects the fees you pay. So check your categories regularly to ensure they're all still optimal. Tracking tools are available to help; many are designed to track category rankings but also alert you to category changes.

---

488 million products
are sold on Amazon's U.S. site. Don't expect them to correctly categorize everything without help.[12]

If you don't feel your product has been assigned correctly — for example, your decorative antique goldpan has been placed in Cookware and Baking Supplies — contact Seller Support and make the case for where it should be instead.

How can you tell, if it's not as obvious as the goldpan example? Perform searches on a few of your most obvious keywords. On the results pages, check which parent nodes appear in the browse navigation menus at the left of the screen. The top five will be most relevant categories for the keyword you searched. Your product needs to be in at least one of those top five.

Tip: Watch category fees.
Categories are assigned various referral fees on each sale, usually between 6 (or, more commonly, 8) and 15 percent. Minimum fees of $1 per item sold typically apply, too. Amazon often changes these fee levels — as you might suspect, mostly upward — so tracking your categories is also important to know what you'll be

---

[12] Grey, Paul. "How Many Products Does Amazon Sell?", Dec. 11, 2015, http://export-x.com/2015/12/11/how-many-products-does-amazon-sell-2015/

paying, particularly if you have products with fairly narrow margins.

Amazon provides a fee preview report that addresses referral fees, FBA fees, and the media category's "variable closing fee." It doesn't include monthly storage fees, and the report doesn't indicate which category fee percentage you'll pay, so you have to manually calculate if a category change is bumping you to a higher fee level and potentially a big competitive disadvantage. As noted above, you can request a change of categories to help control fees, but Amazon may or may not agree and comply with your request.

Ultimately, the effect of product category on keywords and search results placement, and thus sales, is more important than its effect on fees, but you need to be aware of those costs to manage profitability.

Monitor category rankings.

As a product's sales increase relative to competing products, its product category ranking should move higher, too. This ranking is less important than how well your product ranks in keyword search results, because relatively few shoppers browse by category. Still, some use a combination of category browsing and searching, and it does appear that high category rankings are a factor in improving search ranking.

Track this ranking over time and correlate sales, promotional, and inventory events with changes in category ranking. Those changes can be your biggest clue to behind-the-scenes shifts in Amazon algorithms that might warrant a review of your keywords and advertising plans. Ranking changes may also alert you to new competitors or competing products pushing yours off the top of the hill.

Tool Description: Category Ranking Tool

As important as it is to watch category ranking to be aware of algorithm changes or competitors, tracking this metric manually is

> time-consuming and inefficient; plus, manual tracking doesn't give you a look at the bigger picture. Efficient Era's category ranking charts let you track all your products' category rankings with ease to see trends over time. You can also add contextual events to your charts to easily pinpoint which changes are having which effects in the ranking.

10. Prepare to actively combat the "cold-start" problem.

In the introduction, we mentioned what Amazon calls the "cold-start" problem. Previous sales are such a big part of Amazon's algorithm for search visibility, that before you've made any sales, shoppers can't find your product... so you can't make any sales.

It's a Catch-22 that can only be overcome with sustained effort to drive visitors to your product page, both from inside and outside the marketplace, and convince them to buy.

> **Definition: The cold-start problem**
> A new product needs sales and reviews to show up anywhere near the top of search results, but no one can find it to buy until it starts showing up in the search results. That's the downside to the flywheel effect: a lot of inertia to overcome in the beginning. Amazon calls this the cold-start problem.

There are a variety of tactics for overcoming this problem. You can get the e-commerce flywheel moving by:

- Ensuring your product page converts shoppers to customers.
- Participating in Sponsored Products advertising and other promotional activities, both inside and outside of the marketplace, to begin making sales.
- Closing feedback loops with your customers — answering questions, sending order confirmations that encourage them to leave reviews, and responding constructively to seller feedback, for instance — to kickstart reviews and begin increasing your product's relevance in organic searches.

- Managing your product and business over time, as the market and conditions change, to keep the flywheel moving. This includes avoiding anything — such as stock-outs — that will bring the flywheel to a halt and make you start over.

You'll need not one but all of these approaches to successfully launch the great products you're planning to sell.

Chapter 3 —
How to List Products for High Conversions

Shoppers love online marketplaces partly because all the information they need to make a decision can be at their fingertips — far more than in a typical retail environment. There's room for reviews, use tips, accessories, and the answers to questions.

The flip side for sellers is that purchase decisions depend even more on that product information, so it'd better be good. Unfortunately, many businesses with e-commerce stores link to Amazon but don't give their detail pages sufficient care. As a result, they're inadequate.

Don't settle for a sub-par product page. If you do, you'll not only lose sales — you'll ultimately make your product much harder to find and suffer poorer returns when you do advertise. (See the section on keywords and the flywheel for more insight on why.) So once you've settled on your product category, use that virtual space to your greatest advantage and ensure your listings work as hard as possible with thoughtful product page setup.

Refer to the section called "Understanding Amazon Categories" to be sure you list yours in the right browse to enable success. Once you've identified that category, download the category style guide from Amazon. These contain category specific requirements as well as good and bad examples of the various components of a product listing.

1. Hone your product title — especially those first few words.
It's not easy to create a good product title because three opposing criteria come into play:

- **Easy to read and understand** at a glance. Some search views may show as few as the first 24 characters of your title. This tends to imply short and conversational.
- **Highlight what's different** about your product, such as thread count or type of buttons
- **Contain as many strong keywords as possible** to ensure good search results placement.

Trying to accomplish both the second and third above tends to create fairly long titles; it's a matter of how far you abandon the first criteria. Amazon's hard limits on title length can vary by department. 50 characters are always allowed.[13] 150 characters or more are common.

Use them up. It's counter to traditional marketing axioms, but there's no glory in a short, succinct product title online. You're not creating anything that has to be memorable. Titles are one of the places search keywords are drawn from.

Walk the tightrope by giving special attention to the first handful of words and then making good use of all your remaining characters, too. Just do it in a way that's easy to read, with a rhythm, where each slightly longer version of the title makes sense when read as a whole, yet trying to avoid a run-on list of individual adjectives.

Put yourself — or your thirteen-year-old — in the customer's shoes. Include keywords buyers might search for, which might touch on the product use, color, target user, or size. "Boy's thick cotton tank top, four-pack" is a better title than "Boy's tank top." If you need ideas, steal from your competitors.

But remember that only the beginning of the title shows in search results, especially on shoppers' mobile devices. That particularly

---

[13] Amazon: http://tinyurl.com/hkavxqv

becomes a challenge for accessory products that need to list compatibilities as quickly as possible to prevent shoppers from dismissing them.

> # 30% of online retail shopping
> in the U.S. is performed on a mobile device.[14]

This means that you may have only a half-dozen words to encourage the buyer to click on your product. The number of whole words that fit into 40 characters seems to be a frequent cutoff point.

So give special attention to that first handful of words. Make them convey as much as possible about your product, and then make good use of all your remaining characters, too. To do so, know what your customers want. For some products, the color — frequently near the beginning of titles — might be crucial. For others, not so much.

Reconsider putting your brand name as the first word in the product title.

Many sellers list every one of their products with the brand name first. This is an oft-advised strategy that doesn't necessarily make sense for private label sellers.

The brand should definitely be in the title — just not always in the first few words. If you have high brand recognition that drives purchase decisions, it might be wise. But especially if your brand name is long, those precious characters may be wasted on shoppers who care more about features and price. Only you can decide. Do so thoughtfully, not out of habit or ego.

Reconsider the value of a model number early in the product title.

As with the brand name, the model number might make sense there. But how many shoppers have already done their research and are

---

[14] *Internet Retailer*, Aug. 18, 2015, www.internetretailer.com/2015/08/18/mobile-commerce-now-30-all-us-e-commerce

looking for your model number — compared to those who just want the gizmo at a competitive price?

Plus, shoppers who know they want the WhizBanger Industries 6003-R Multi-Channel Doodad will probably keep looking until they find it, even if 6003-R is the *last* word of the title. They might even type 6003-R in their searches. In that case, no worries — yours will display high on the list, if not first. But customers who don't know your 6003-R may click the first search result or ad that says "doodad."

Make sure it's *your* doodad they explore further. Get "Doodad" in the first three or four words, whether 6003-R is or not.

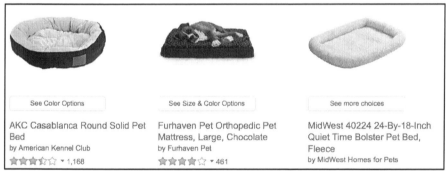

Compare these product titles. Which says the most? How relatively valuable is the brand, model name or number, or size in helping a customer make a choice to click?

Think about your title in coherent segments.

As noted above, you never know how much of your title will be displayed after a search. So develop your title in two or three logical chunks, starting with no more than 40 characters. Come up with a very short version that is true and complete (if not comprehensive) and then add details in logical order — with increasing detail — so you've got both a single intelligible title that also stands alone at "medium" and "long" lengths, too. Here's an example:

- Shortest version: Rubber barn boots, unisex, fleece-lined
- Medium version: Rubber barn boots, unisex, fleece-lined, mid-calf with pull-on handles, six designer colors

- Long version: Rubber barn boots, unisex, fleece-lined, mid-calf with pull-on handles, six designer colors for adults and kids
- Full product page title: Rubber barn boots, unisex, fleece-lined, mid-calf with pull-on handles, six designer colors for adults and kids, non-skid treads for wet muck plus removable, fast-dry liners with anti-sweat fabric

Revisit the title and get other opinions.
Is "unisex" better in the example above than "men, women, kids"? It's shorter, but it may be less effective. Look at Amazon search suggestions (known as search hints), make changes and run tests, and track data from your keyword advertising to identify the title keywords customers will use and care about most.

Tip: Hear the customer's voice, not Product Development's.
One successful electronics seller often puts model numbers near the end of titles. "I have to fight my product managers' inclinations," says the seller. "Technically minded people often want to put a model number first because it's a precise way of describing the product. Instead, we try to read shoppers' minds about what they already know about such products and what they think they want when they start searching. We do better when we put those few critical words up front."

---

2. Display a better main product image than your competitors.
Make a good first impression. Whether in an ad or organic search results, the first image desktop shoppers will see of your product is about the size of a Wheat Thin cracker. If they're using their phones — as a growing proportion do — it'll be closer to the size of a fingernail.

Almost 70%
of Amazon's 2015 holiday shoppers used a mobile device.[15]

But your product photo must speak for itself; plenty of shoppers buy on the image alone, without reading a word but the price.

So follow Amazon's image guidelines and upload professional-quality photos, even if you take them yourself. In particular:

- Shoot high-resolution with adequate lighting for sharp, beautiful images and true colors.
- Size your main product image at a minimum of 1000 pixels on one side (with a maximum of 1500 on the longest). For some categories, this enables zoom, which demonstrably improves sales.[16]
- Follow the white-background rule to focus customers on the product (and avoid having your photos rejected).

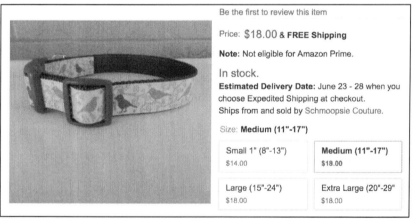

Avoid this: A poor main image is likely to eventually be removed by Amazon.

- Show the product, not the front of the package it comes in.

---

[15] Amazon press release, Dec. 28, 2015, http://phoenix.corporate-ir.net/phoenix.zhtml?c=176060&p=irol-newsArticle&ID=2125057
[16] Amazon: http://tinyurl.com/j896euh

- Crop tightly and use the whole space, edge to edge, so the product's as large as possible. Amazon specifies a minimum of 85% of the space, but aim higher. For weirdly-shaped products, use creativity to find an angle that is both clear and doesn't result in a lot of empty white space.

This image uses space and displays product features more clearly than the previous one.

- If at all possible, show the product so that your logo and/or brand name are clear (preferably integrated into the product, rather than as a label). This can help discourage hijackers.

Including the brand identity can help dissuade counterfeiters.

- Correct images as needed to eliminate shadows or glare.

- Don't be afraid to invest in help. Photographers who specialize in Amazon product photography are neither expensive nor hard to find.
- Bank on "better late than never." Unfortunately, when products are first launched, sellers are often in a rush. If you need a few iterations to end up with great photos, do it. Upload better images as soon as you can. The effort will pay off in more sales.

Blueberry Pet 3/4-Inch Summer Nautical Flags Inspired Designer Basic Polyester Nylon Dog Collar, Medium
by Blueberry Pet

★★★★☆ ▾ 218

$12.99 $15.45 ✓Prime

Get it by **Saturday, Jun 18**

Product Features
... The *dog collars* in the first main picture are sold separately; And ...

Pet Supplies: See all 316,825 items

Avoid this: The features text wastes keywords when it has to say, "The collars in the main picture are sold separately." And which of these collars matches the title's "nautical flags" reference?

Get multiple images, upload the best, and be willing to shoot and upload them again later. Product launches often involve a rush, and it can take several iterations to get the photo just right. But it's easy to find lousy product images online; make yours better to leap over a large percentage of your competition.

---

45 million U.S. adults
are functionally illiterate; some estimates are as high as 23 percent of the population. They shop on Amazon, too.[17]

---

3. Take advantage of the ability to show multiple images.

Amazon knows images sell. The number you can show on your product listing, as well as the amount of text and other listing content,

---

[17] Literacy Project Foundation, http://literacyprojectfoundation.org/community/statistics/

such as PDFs, varies by category and undergoes constant testing and tweaking. Some limitations depend on the seller's relationship to Amazon, too, or seller participation in Vendor Central, for instance. Expect the limitations to keep changing, but for now, Amazon allows a maximum of 9 images in most categories because they know photos sell. Use them effectively in a variety of product views. For instance:

- Indicate scale.
- Show the product from the back, sides, or other relevant angles.
- Provide close-ups for features such as texture, fasteners, controls, use options, handles, connections or ports, etc.
- Show the main product with accompanying parts, cases, or accessories.
- Display the product it its packaging, when it can clarify information such as size, inclusions, or quality.
- Consider the risk/benefit ratio of including non-photographic additions to your main images, from certifications to compatibility information. This is an example of pushing the envelope on policies. You may get away with it, at least in specific Amazon marketplaces or for a time; you may find the images deleted or the listing suspended. Only you can decide if the value of providing that information to consumers as part of the image might outweigh the risks.

Convey all the important characteristics of the product that may influence the buying decision. Don't be redundant, though. It annoys shoppers to click through similar photos to see the few that are different. Find angles and details worth showing.

Include a lifestyle shot of a happy customer with the product in its native environment. Among other things, such an image displays the product's scale and offers application ideas.

Finally, in some categories, Amazon has begun offering sellers additional text and images — for a fee. Depending on your product, this might be a good investment. Especially for costly purchases, additional images and information can be compelling.

What about video?

Not long ago, videos represented the hot new technique for attracting attention — if your sales volume was high enough for Amazon to enable the option. It hasn't always been easy for most sellers to get the attention of the right Amazon managers to make the request, but there are indicators that video is effective; look for more options to come. Particularly for a product that requires assembly, includes accessories, or can be showcased in a wide range of uses, a video can improve both sales and product reviews.

---

4. Craft your product description and feature bullets carefully.

Look at the competition. How do they describe competing or similar products? Based on the text on their product pages, which would you buy?

This is not rocket science. Simply strive to see product pages through the eyes of a shopper. Hear the customer's voice. Try to (correctly) predict which words people will search for so that if your product appears, they will click, buy — and be happy. Remember, when selecting keywords, your goal is not to have millions of eyeballs trained on your product page. It's to have *only* eyeballs matched with fingers that click to buy.

Make optimum use of the feature bullets — the second place search keywords are drawn from — by working in your best keywords. Don't waste characters by repeating keywords from your title. Instead, add coordinating keywords to give customers certainty your product is the one they want.

Make the bullets easy to read, not a mere list of keywords. This is a good place to craft copy that sounds conversational while making clever use of alternate keywords for describing the same thing.

Roper

Roper Men's Barn Boot

 ▾   52 customer reviews |
3 answered questions

Price: **$55.77 - $71.99** & FREE Returns. Details
Sale: Lower price available on select options

Fit: As expected (55%) ▾

Size:

Select ▾ Size Chart

Color: Black

- 100% Rubber
- Imported
- Rubber sole
- Shaft measures approximately 13" from arch
- Boot opening measures approximately 16.5" around
- Neoprene upper
- Flexible sole
- 13 inch upper
- Muck

Compare this product title and features with the next...

Which seller makes better use of the product title and feature bullets? The first product repeats words, leaves available characters and keywords unused, and (although you can't tell from the screenshot) ignores features evident in the product photo. The second product sells with robust features that continue down the page.

Think also about which words people might use to search when they are *not* looking for your product but could get confused. You don't want your hand-made sock puppets to appear in a search for gym socks, because your conversion metrics would be terrible. To avoid that, think about how to express the flavor, style, uses, construction, or professionalism level of your product. Sock puppet sellers might consider keywords such as handmade, funny, googlie-eyes, and knit, not to mention puppet, puppet show, craft, entertaining, etc., while staying away from "gym," "men's," "women's" and even "kid's" at all costs.

Share your draft copy with others to get fresh eyes on it and help catch typos or grammatical errors. Shoppers may assume that errors in your product description mean your product quality is shoddy, too.

Similarly, beware overselling — from exclamation points to "greatest ever" hyperbole. It's a universal turn-off that will make shoppers mistrust you. Stick to product features, uses, and demonstrable benefits, and let great reviews handle the exclamation points for you.

5. Be scientific about entering your "hidden" keywords.

In addition to the product title and feature bullets (and product description, for categories that draw keywords from there), Amazon offers sellers five lengthy fields in which to enter additional keywords. Keywords are the focus of *lots* of online advice, not all of it wise. A few high points to follow:

- Put as many keywords in each of the five entry lines as you can. The character limit changes and in the past has varied by browse node, but with the limits not always documented. To make matters worse, if you went over the limit or included a character that wasn't permitted, the Amazon system provided no error messages — it just stopped processing anything after the problem. Sellers didn't even know that not all their keyword entries were used.

  In Spring 2016, some analysts reported new limits of up to 1,000 characters per field.[18] For a time, that expansion seemed to vary by browse node and sometimes reverted back to 50 characters per field, based on API upload error reporting. As of

---

[18] For example, see CPC Strategy, http://www.cpcstrategy.com/blog/2016/02/amazon-search-terms-increases-character-limits-1000/ ; also Brian Johnson, http://www.ampmpodcast.com/interview-amazon-ppc-expert-brian-johnson-joins-manny-coats-value-packed-interview-ep37/

this writing, 1,000 characters seems to have become standard, but about the best you can do is try to find recent documentation from Amazon of the character limit for your browse node and either stick with that limit or experiment with longer entries using API submission so you'll get error codes if you go over. You can always do searches on keywords late on your list to see if they seem to be linked to your product or not. Efficient Era's tools will also help find any errors, including keywords that are not applying because of length limits.

- Amazon suggests putting the terms in likely search order, but there's not much evidence that it matters. Pay even less attention to the Amazon example, which shows unnecessary commas between keywords. Commas waste characters you could use for another keyword. Just separate your keywords (or the words in a keyword combination) by a space.
- Don't waste characters by entering the product title, EAN/UPC, manufacturer, or merchant, which are all automatic keywords.
- To identify keywords, start with Amazon's search feature itself. Enter the most important noun in your product name. Above the dividing line, Amazon suggests the top relevant categories, which all contain positively associated keywords. Below the dividing line are the top related searches — what Amazon calls "search hints" — that began with the same word. Steal appropriate keywords from those suggestions.

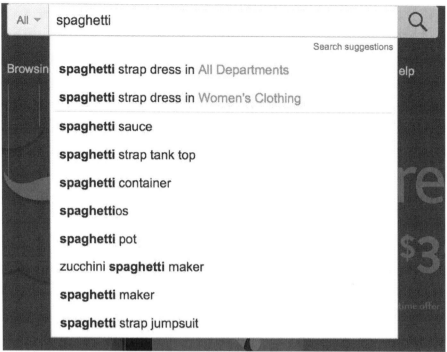

Search hints, which are the top related searches for the beginning of a search string, are a good source of keywords that may be appropriate.

- Don't repeat words. Instead of entering, "dog bed cat bed pet bed" in your hidden search field, enter "dog cat pet bed" (and use the rest of your characters wisely). For organic search results, the system will treat each word discretely, mixing and matching with abandon. *Note that the same is not true when you're bidding on keywords for Sponsored Products advertising unless you elect the broad search type.*
- The search system does a little simple aliasing — for instance, displaying a product with the keyword "blankets" even if the shopper typed "blanket," or "girl" if the shopper typed "girl's." But don't count on that. To the extent possible without sacrificing other important keywords, include multiple versions in your hidden keyword fields.
- Don't assume you can think of all the right keywords yourself, at least not to start. Fortunately, there are lots of tools that can

help you identify and include vital keywords, and you can change those keywords as often as you like.

6. Use as many of the product characteristics fields as apply.

Every department has a schema of potential characteristics associated with it, from size and color to very specific category references such as, for bath tissue, the number of rolls in a package. Fill in information for as many of these product characteristics as you can. When you do, you'll ensure your product can be included when shoppers use the filter options to narrow their search results.

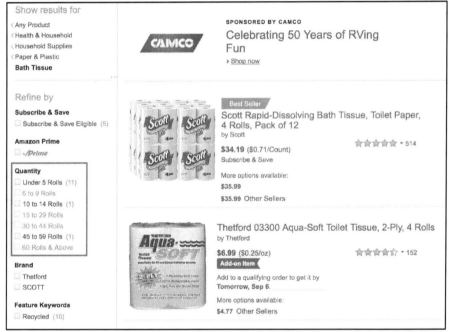

Take advantages of category-specific characteristics that may not display in the product listing but that are used by search filters and the algorithm.

7. Manage your catalog proactively.

As you launch a product, be prepared to change titles and keywords frequently — as much as every few days to start — until your keyword advertising data and sales suggest that you're what you're doing is working. (See the section on keywords and the flywheel for details.)

Don't stop after the launch, though. Take advantage of online product information — far easier to update than packaging or product manuals — by managing it to maximize sales. That means treating it like a living entity and changing it as often as you can reasonably manage. There's always work to clarify, correct, or update product details, pricing, and specs — not to mention incorporating more effective keywords and ideas for how customers can use the product based on insights and ideas in the product reviews.

If you can, update your product listings to reflect seasonality, current events, and new trends. Localize it (such as by converting imperial units to metric or vice versa) whenever you expand to a new market. Yes, this means more management time, which is multiplied if you're working across different marketplaces and languages. That's why something seemingly as simply as catalog management trips up many companies: Outdated information on product detail pages often results in an uptick in support and refund requests, as well as an unknown effect in lost sales.

Good tools can take on a lot of the burden — and reduce errors — by automating updates, handling localization, and replicating changes across geographies. At minimum, create a gigantic spreadsheet with a tab for each product, and enter product detail information in the appropriate languages for your various markets. Scripts can then automatically make localizations and send the updates to Amazon's different geographies.

Efficient Era

Chapter 4 —
How to Get the Flywheel Moving

An awful lot of webinars, podcasts, and consultants focus on improving search results, optimizing keywords, and chasing the latest "new Amazon secret" as algorithms, policies, and marketplace features change.

While these tactics have value, they're missing the forest for the trees. Focus first on creating a good product, with the features people want, at a competitive price, and with good service attached.

That said, particularly for new products, getting the flywheel moving and keeping it humming can seem like a chicken/egg dilemma: You need sales to appear high enough in search results to attract shoppers, but until they can find you, it's hard to make sales. Amazon calls it the cold-start problem.

How do you overcome that inertia and make the system work for you? Four related factors affect sales inertia:

- **Relevance**. This is an assessment by Amazon's search function about how perfectly your product will match what the buyer is looking for. That is, if a customer types "shoestring," do they want your superior lacings for holding sneakers on feet, or are they actually after a fried potato snack or a type of licorice? Or perhaps a very skinny tie, a shoestring alternative such as plastic shoe closers, or a book about traveling on a shoestring?

It's a mind-reading game in which Amazon makes educated guesses. Though only the algorithm knows for sure, the evidence suggests that relevance scoring is a complex calculation based on, at minimum, category and keywords, sales ranking, reviews, and price — if not, in fact, all the data Amazon has, from the average time shoppers spend on your page to the number of images on it.

- **Discoverability**. If the customer *does* want sneaker laces, does your product listing appear somewhere near the top of the search results, so the customer can notice and click on it?
- **Conversion rate**. If the customer wants sneaker laces *and* clicks on your product page, do the features, price, and product reviews convince them to buy?
- **The customer experience**. If customers buy your sneaker laces, do they love them and the service that supplied them? Amazon uses the answers to influence discoverability.

The Amazon sales funnel, which is shaped by discoverability, relevance, conversions, and the customer experience.

These four factors are interdependent. Discoverability and conversion are the chicken and egg, since strong sales are rewarded with higher search rankings. But relevance and conversion rates are reciprocal, too. Higher relevance increases conversion rates. (Weird search results cause frustration, not sales, and the notion that "at least you're getting exposure" is false in the online sales model. See the following section for more about that.)

Less intuitively, the reverse is true, too: Conversion rates can affect relevance. If shoppers click "Buy now" more often for you than for your competitor, your product becomes more relevant for the search term. And if enough people type "shoestring," and then find and buy your "shoestring" bikini, the Amazon machine will decide shoestring is a valid search term for a swimsuit. The relevance of that term will increase for the category, and search results will increasingly display bikinis alongside shoelaces and fried potatoes, because sales have demonstrated that's what some searchers are looking to buy.

Relevance is subject to shifts when new products or sellers come along, innovation results in a new way to do things — like replace shoestrings with magnets — or when new language or slang becomes associated with a product through cultural references.

Finally, even conversions aren't the end of the story, since customer reviews influence future discoverability, either goosing or putting the brakes on sales momentum. This is good because it forces the cream to the top and encourages sellers to make customers happy, which is in everyone's best interests. (See the sections of this guide on product reviews and seller feedback.)

The effect of feedback on relevance is also a huge advantage of the Amazon system over Google's. Google's system reports on impressions and clicks, but its ability to subsequently identify conversions is imprecise at best. Advertisers can get a much better sense of the effectiveness of keywords used on Amazon than on Google, and this is true for both paid and organic searches.

Definition: Organic search

"Organic search" has nothing to do with a lack of pesticides. It refers to what happens when a shopper searches an online marketplace. A product is displayed because it has keywords that match the search terms — though only products with great sales and good reviews show up near the top of a very long list.

The opposite of organic search is paid advertising, in which a product is displayed because a) it has keywords that match *and* b) the seller was among the highest bidders for one or more keywords in the search. There are probably c) other factors, such as product ratings, as well, but much of the system is a black box for sellers, so we have to fall back on evidence and the logic that seems to underlie it, adjusting when results suggest something has changed.

Three strategies for escaping the chicken/egg conundrum

When everything affects everything else, how do you get the flywheel moving in what's been dubbed the "virtuous cycle?" From the moment your product launches, you need to train Amazon's artificial intelligence that your product is a high converter for given keywords. In other words, make sales based on searches using those words.

If it were only that easy. Plus Amazon constantly changes the rules, partly to help prevent gaming of the system. Still, a few fundamental strategies help customers, Amazon, and sellers alike. Use a three-pronged approach, listed here in no particular order because they must be addressed simultaneously:

- **Ensure your product page converts well** by pricing competitively, getting a good review rating, and optimizing other page content. Pricing is beyond the scope of this guide, and reviews are addressed in other sections, so we'll focus here on optimization.
- **Increase relevance**. Get eyeballs on that optimized product page through marketplace promotion, including Amazon Sponsored Products advertising. Paid ads that convert are

crucial for training the search function and building your product's relevance for your keywords.

- **Make sales**. No kidding, right? But don't rely on organic discovery; there won't be any. Get traffic going to your product page through external promotion, and then take steps to ensure those visitors become happy customers who help convince others to buy.

A variety of tactics can help you accomplish each, and progress in one helps drive the others. That's the virtuous cycle at work.

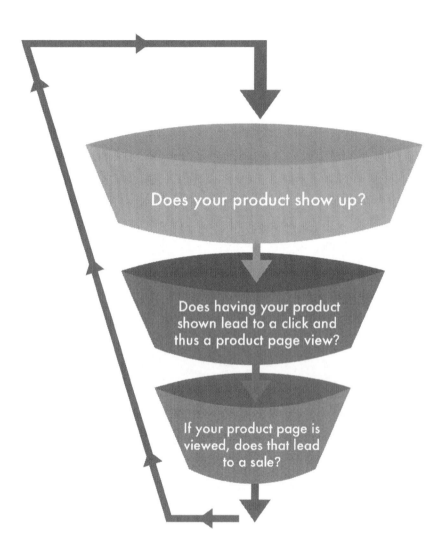

The Amazon sales funnel is a virtuous cycle, since every click and every sale helps your product show up more often, ushering more shoppers into the top of the funnel.

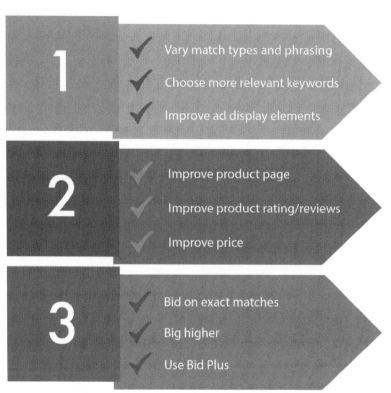

But before you can do a good job on any of these, it's crucial to understand the nuances of using keywords. That's because keywords are one of your more practical levers for moving shoppers into the sales funnel.

First: Understand keywords and how to capitalize on them.
Sellers often think of keywords as "Amazon SEO," but it's important to recognize critical differences from Google SEO. For starters,

Amazon's search engine is more simplistic.[19] More importantly, it serves a different function, so a different approach is required to capitalize on it.

A keyword by any other name

"Keyword" is a bit of a misnomer, since it actually may be words in a phrase. For organic search, the distinction doesn't matter. For Sponsored Products ad displays, it does. The term is still used to describe one or more words you are bidding on as a unit. "Bike" is a keyword. "Red bike" may be, too, with "bike red" representing a separate keyword in exact-match campaigns.

---

1. Realize that recent sales are heavily weighted.

People use Google or other search engines for all kinds of reasons, including research, entertainment, and shopping. People who search on Amazon are either ready to buy, based on a need, or doing research just prior to purchase. That's why the Amazon algorithm weights recent sales heavily. It makes the probably valid assumption that if a bunch of recent customers decided on the Acme Thingamajig, the next person searching with the same words probably will, too.

So regardless of how many of your product's keywords match the search, if your product is not selling, it won't rank well in results. Other weighted factors include price competitiveness and seller performance metrics. (The latter are increasingly used to filter the search results, kicking sellers with low metrics down in the rankings.)

In general, the search algorithm weights factors you want to keep strong anyway, if you want your business to last. Still, Amazon puts the burden on you to make sure your product is found when it should be. That means success really comes down to:

- **How** the customer describes the solution to her need
- **If** your product is in fact the solution she's looking for.

---

[19] More at http://www.ecomengine.com/blog/serp-and-seo/

Once you take that mindset, you can ignore any "tricks" and focus on just two things: the product and your ideal customer.

2. Know your product.

This sounds obvious! But it's easy to overlook potential keywords, both on your product page and in your advertising. So when you consider keywords, keep in mind:

- Product functionalities
- Product compatibilities
- Product uses
- Product seasonality, if any
- Competitors' products and your differentiators
- Things your product is *not* and words that will help you indicate that.

There's no point in making your product sound like something it's not; that'll only draw lousy product reviews. And it's a waste of money to make people searching for X aware of your Y. In particular, don't include competitors' brand names in your keywords, either on the product page or for Sponsored Products advertising. Amazon considers this a form of inappropriate search manipulation that can result in account suspension.[20]

> **Tip: Shun keyword shenanigans.**
> Google has been more sophisticated than Amazon about blocking attempts to game the system by, for instance, keyword loading. This is especially evident when searching for a branded item or book title on Amazon — sometimes the results are head-scratchers, usually as a result of ploys by unscrupulous sellers. Don't be tempted by tricks, because Amazon will likely catch up eventually. In the meantime, don't be naïve, but do the right thing for customers and present your product with their best interests in mind. In the long run, satisfying them will butter your own bread.

---

[20] Amazon: http://tinyurl.com/jf8fhtw

3. Anticipate the customer.

Anticipating how people *think and talk about their needs* isn't just important for your product development team; it's crucial to turning shoppers into customers.

What do customers want? How do they type those desires in the search field? How often are others doing the same or similar searches? When people are shown your product, how likely are they to see it as the solution they need? If they do click through and read the details, do they take the leap to buy? The answers are crucial to turning Amazon shoppers into *your* customers.

Why keywords are important

The virtuous cycle plays out both for organic searches and in pay per click (PPC) or pay per sale realms such as Sponsored Products advertising. In some ways, they're separate systems, and Amazon splits shopper attention between organic results and ads sold to the highest relevant bidder. But both systems start with the search and hinge on keywords — and Amazon uses results from each system as feedback that affects the other.

A product might have dozens or even hundreds of relevant keywords. Some will be better — more likely to lead to a sale — than others.

Make high ranking in organic searches your ultimate goal. Because your success with keywords is so crucial to that goal, use Sponsored Products advertising as a primary technique to achieve it. This "paid search" system trains the organic system about which products are most relevant for a given keyword. That means that even a keyword that's dead for organic search — that is, it wouldn't result in your product being displayed — can be animated if you buy a paid ad for it and prove that it's relevant by making sales from that ad. That's important, especially when your products are launching.

Before you can advertise, however, you need to create product listings, so most sellers first tussle with keywords when creating listings. As a result, identifying, testing, and refining keywords is an iterative process that starts, but doesn't end, with keywords in your listing.

Second: Optimize the keywords in your product listing

The section of this guide about creating product listings contains lots of best practices; now is a good time to review them. The most important for building search relevance involve your product category, your product title, and the visible and "hidden" keywords in your listing.

Keyword sources

When a shopper uses Amazon search, the search phrase is compared with keywords from these sources:

- Category-associated keywords
- Product title
- Product feature bullets
- The meta-field or "hidden" keywords sellers can select when listing the product

Product descriptions *may or may not* be a keyword source; it depends on the category. Consider testing to know for certain. Then use the keyword sources that are in your control wisely.

---

1. Make certain you're in the right category (or categories).

As noted in the section on Understanding Amazon, categories can change without notice, so keep tabs on your category and be certain it's right. This is important because the keywords associated with categories are cumulative. If your product is in multiple relevant categories, those categories' "automatic" keywords can boost your search placement. But if a category's keywords don't result in good conversions, their cumulative impact will be negative. So get your product in the relevant category or categories — and stop there.

2. Refine your product title.

The keywords in titles appear to be weighted most heavily, so make great use of your allotted characters. But don't forget that many search results and marketplace widgets, such as "Customers who bought this item also bought…," will only show the first half-dozen words. How much shoppers see is also affected by their devices.

> ## 30% of online retail shopping
> in the U.S. is performed on a mobile device.[21]

Not only that, but Amazon frequently changes the page locations and space allotted for various elements, and the page is only likely to get more crowded. Sometimes more words will show, and sometimes it'll be only the number of whole words that fit into about 40 characters. These limitations can be a particular challenge for accessory products that need to list compatibilities quickly to prevent shoppers from dismissing them.

In short, think hard about those first words and ensure they reflect what your customers actually search for.

3. Keep refining your visible and hidden keywords.

Assume your keywords will need continual improvement. You probably won't have included all of the best ones to start. Plus a remarkable number of people search on "long tail" keywords, such as "shoestring" for a skimpy bikini.[22] In fact, so many use odd keywords that, year in and year out, some 15 percent of Google searches each day are unique — never before searched.[23] Amazon searches, because they relate exclusively to something a shopper wants to buy, may not involve quite so many new keywords and combinations, but the principle likely holds: It's almost impossible to accurately predict how people *who aren't you* may think.

---

[21] *Internet Retailer*, Aug. 18, 2015, www.internetretailer.com/2015/08/18/mobile-commerce-now-30-all-us-e-commerce, and Jan. 6, 2016, www.internetretailer.com/2016/01/06/mobile-devices-deliver-holiday-e-commerce-sales

[22] Scientific Seller: http://app.scientificseller.com/keywordtool

[23] Farber, Dan, "Google Search Scratches Its Brain 500 Million Times a Day," CNET, May 13, 2013. http://www.cnet.com/news/google-search-scratches-its-brain-500-million-times-a-day/ Also Mitchell, Jon, "How Google Search Really Works," *ReadWrite*, Feb. 29, 2012, http://readwrite.com/2012/02/29/interview_changing_engines_mid-flight_qa_with_goog/#awesm=%7EoiNkM4tAX3xhbP

So be continually on the alert for new keywords that ought to replace low performers in your product listing. Think also about words in your listing that might unintentionally mislead shoppers. You don't want your handmade sock puppets to appear in a search for gym socks, because your conversion metrics would be terrible. To avoid that, consider how to express the flavor, style, uses, construction, or professionalism level of your product. A sock puppet seller might consider keywords such as handmade, funny, googlie-eyes, and personality, not to mention puppet, puppet show, craft, entertaining, etc., while staying away from "gym," "men," and "women" at all costs.

> **Tip: Remember that sales count way more than impressions.**
> Your goal is not merely to show up in a search but to prompt that shopper to click through and buy.

As you make changes, coordinate your entries for the keyword sources to ensure that between them you have no redundancy waste but do have typical variations or misspellings. When shoppers search, your product appears, and they buy, you generate evidence that your product is highly relevant for those keywords, so it'll show up more often next time and the "virtuous cycle" kicks in. Test to ensure that a new entry improves your search ranking or other metrics.

The bad news is that such testing is time-consuming, and Amazon doesn't give a "search ranking" report — you'd need a tool that can scrape those results for you.

The good news is that there's an easier way to test keywords: Sponsored Products advertising. See the next major section for more about this big topic.

4. Use the ASIN report to identify opportunities for improvement.
Amazon's "Detail Page Sales and Traffic by ASIN" report indicates how many people have viewed your product and how many of those resulted in sales. That conversion rate is critical. It helps identify

whether you're getting exposure and simply not converting, or aren't being found in the first place, so you can respond accordingly.

Pull your ASIN reports regularly, if not daily, and use them to create 30-day snapshots of products that aren't converting well over time. Then target those products for improvement. Consider improving the listing, reducing the price (at least temporarily), or advertising to drive more relevant traffic. If those tactics don't work, consider eliminating those products. See the Troubleshooting section for more about this.

G	H	I
Page Views	Page Views P	Buy Box Perc
25,051	8.84%	100%
1,451	0.51%	100%
167	0.06%	99%
2,172	0.77%	100%
9,373	3.31%	100%
268	0.09%	100%
1,537	0.54%	100%

J	K	L
Units Ordered	Units Ordered	Unit Session
79	0	0.34%
6	0	0.46%
1	0	0.67%
17	0	0.88%
78	1	0.93%
3	1	1.31%
23	0	1.78%

Products with low conversion rates on ASIN reports need attention to their product pages, keywords, or ad campaigns.

When you're confident — again — that your keywords are ideal, the next step is product promotion.

Third: Increase relevance by driving traffic to your product page.

Quick review: To get the flywheel moving, you'll want to:

- Optimize page content, including keywords.
- Increase relevance.
- Make sales and get good reviews.

Check off that first one: You've got a product page that sells. Great! But you could launch the best product in the world, one that everyone desperately needs, with the ideal listing and price. If you do nothing else, your great product will fail because no one will ever find it. There's too much noise in the system. If anyone is ever to see your product, you've got to build relevance by moving your sales metrics.

A fun game (not for the easily depressed)
When you first launch a new product, try to find it on Amazon once it's listed but before you've begun promoting it. Good luck. It's hard, even with plenty of sweat on your keywords. To make it appear in early search results, you have to be extremely specific and include the brand in your search, because from Amazon's perspective, your product has no relevance at all.

Imagine your product on page 400 of the search results. Not even your mother will click "Next page" that many times.

One strategy for making sales and building relevance in organic searches is to drive traffic to your Amazon product page, from outside the marketplace, with external promotion. But online marketplaces require a mental shift about what promotion is for.

1. Update your concept of what promotion achieves.
Unlike, say, television advertising, online marketing is not about tempting people, helping them remember your name, or playing on their egos or fears to persuade them to buy something they otherwise

wouldn't want. It's not even about making people aware your product exists.

It's about **anticipating customer needs, accurately describing those needs in the customer's words, and narrowly targeting prospective customers who are now or will soon be ready to buy.** General awareness will do you no good.

So plan online promotions to balance two competing factors: You do want to introduce your product to shoppers who don't already know about it. But don't waste time and money promoting to someone who's never going to buy; that will only wreck your conversion rate.

It's like those standardized tests that penalize random guessing — it's better not to answer at all. Similarly, at least for the Amazon platform, it's better not to spend promotional dollars on any shoppers who aren't actively your market. To belabor the example, shoppers looking for shoestring potatoes might click on your shoestring bikini ad to ogle your photos, but the odds of them buying are virtually nil, and the Amazon flywheel doesn't reward entertainment.

2. Promote the product externally to encourage traffic to its Amazon page.
Once your head is on straight regarding promotion, some of the more common approaches include:

- Advertise outside the marketplace, including Google or Facebook. Rather than including a direct link to the Amazon product page in such promotion, it can be wise to channel that traffic via an intermediate landing page, such as a blog or website, where visitors can see more detailed product images and information and essentially be pre-qualified before they click onward to Amazon. This can help limit the harm caused by fake accounts, clickbots, or people with no real interest in your product. You don't want them visiting your Amazon product page and wrecking your conversion metrics.

- Run social media campaigns, from blog posts to YouTube videos, that include links, probably to that intermediate landing page.
- Solicit product announcements and reviews in trade and special-interest publications, online and in print.
- Organize product discounts or giveaways that result in Amazon product reviews. If the discount is greater than 50 percent, they won't be Amazon-verified purchases, but especially to start, those reviews are still well worth getting.
- Any other earned or unearned promotion you can swing in your product niche.

Unfortunately, except for books and movies, external promotion is rarely enough to sufficiently improve product relevance and thus visibility. You'll also need to promote within the marketplace itself.

Super URLs

For a long time, Amazon used a simplistic system to track what searches led to what purchases — they would carry the search terms along in URL parameters.

Some sellers then game the system by sharing these links (they got to be called "super URLs"). When clicked, these links direct browsers to the product page but give the appearance that the shopper used certain search terms to get there — in effect seeding Amazon's data for those keywords.

There's recent evidence that super URLs no longer have any effect, and Amazon reps confirm this, saying, "The short story is 'super URLs' do not impact search results, so we consider them unimportant from a search ranking standpoint."[24] Further, in February 2016 Amazon added new language to its list of prohibited seller activities regarding attempts to manipulate the search experience. Super URLs would probably count. (See the list at http://tinyurl.com/gv8qqcg.)

---

[24] Amazon email, June 14, 2016

> Regardless, in the long run, Sponsored Products advertising and actual customer searches are better for identifying and strengthening effective search terms that customers will use to find your product and buy.

3. Use Amazon Sponsored Products advertising to hone your keywords.

For online marketplaces today, it's only viable to skip in-market advertising if:

- Your product is truly unique *and* you have some other way of making people look for it specifically in organic search.
- You already have brand awareness on the level of Apple iPhones.

Since neither is true for most of us, expect to advertise for most, if not all, of your products. Two key ways paid promotion can help you:

1. **Gain search insight**. Paid promotion is the best way to find out what potential customers search for, and how. Amazon provides advertisers with really good data about whether those keywords were right for that product — if people did in fact search, click, and buy. Do they type "luggage with locks" or "TSA-proof suitcase?"
2. **Increase relevance.** Remember, you need to train Amazon's artificial intelligence that your product is a high converter for given keywords. Paid ads, subsequent shopper clicks, and then sales create evidence that your product should be a trusted, relevant result for those keywords. Ad clicks that don't generate sales will hurt your conversion rate and represent lost advertising pennies. So select the keywords you bid on for advertising thoughtfully.

There's a third benefit, too: It's impossible to understand, let alone influence, the interactions and dependencies between advertising keywords and organic search unless you take them together.

Once you've got some likely keywords — both broad, such as "pet supplies," and narrow, such as "heated dog bed," plan your keyword campaigns with the following steps.

Get ready by identifying metrics. Smart advertising decisions require a few data ingredients:

Know the product's profit margin. Keep direct and category fees in mind to ensure that a campaign doesn't lose money wildly. You may be willing to forgo profit for a while to meet other goals, but don't forget why you're in business.

Know the organic ranking performance to start. A huge benefit of Sponsored Products advertising is its positive effect on the product's category ranking and ranking in organic searches on the same keywords. Comparing those rankings before and during a campaign can help demonstrate whether that campaign is a success. (Tracking tools that can report ranking by keyword can help.)

By the same token, don't bid a lot for keywords where you're already ranking well — in those cases, the flywheel is already working for you, so it's not the best use of your advertising dollar.

Identify campaign goals and a target ACOS. Are you trying to make money? Raise a new product's visibility? Own a particular keyword to improve organic search placement? The goal will influence the advertising cost of sales (ACOS) you're willing to incur, and for how long. Note that ACOS doesn't include direct and category fees, which is why you need to know your margin to determine a wise ACOS.

The top campaign metric: ACOS
To use paid ads effectively, pay attention to each product's advertising cost of sales (ACOS). This term, which is more common in the Amazon world than elsewhere, is the cost of a given sale attributable to the advertising. You can obtain this metric from the Campaign Manager interface. It's also provided in the

---

performance reporting of the Amazon advertising application programming interface (API,) which can save time for sellers who manage large or complex campaigns and who understand the use of APIs.[25]

In traditional markets, you'd rarely allow advertising costs to eat up your entire profit margin, but in online markets, the calculation can be more complex. For new products or those you believe in but that aren't getting traction, plan to incur a high ACOS to get the flywheel spinning. It's well worth the investment. Depending on your margins, consider spending enough for an ACOS of from 20 to 40 percent.

Once the product is established and doing well, you'll want to keep ACOS relatively low. So scale back to a percentage above zero but less than you'd spend at launch. The value of PPC campaigns can vary by category, so experiment with the percentage you need to keep sales momentum from dropping off.

Determine your goals at the keyword level; a given ACOS percentage may represent a huge success for a popular keyword, for which competition is tough, but the same figure may be a poor performance for a long-tail keyword you should be able to own.

Incorporate realistic insight about competitive products that rank organically higher than yours. What can you learn from those sellers? Does their product actually have more features, a better price, or characteristics that relate better to a given keyword than yours? If so, recognize that you may not ever win that top bid or top ranking. That doesn't mean you can't succeed; just plan your goals accordingly.

Use automated keyword campaigns appropriately.
Sellers can choose from two types of Sponsored Ad campaigns: automatic and manual. In an automatic campaign, you empower Amazon to cast a wide keyword net for a maximum advertising spend.

---

[25] http://tinyurl.com/gnve577

Automatic campaigns have very poor conversion rates, but starting here does have two big benefits:

- When you're launching a product, it can help identify the category's top successful keywords, as well as no-brainers you may have missed.
- The targeting report you'll receive from automatic campaigns is the only way to see real customer searches. This report is very helpful for later setting up effective exact match and phrase-match bids for your manual campaigns.

Amazon keyword reports

As of this writing, Amazon provides two reports related to keywords. Their API names are the Sponsored Products "Mega Report" and the "Automatic Targeting Report," a.k.a. the search term report. (The names are slightly different in the online seller control panel.) The most important data to pull from these reports are what keywords shoppers are actually using to search, conversion rates by keyword, and trends.

If you're new to PPC, use an automatic campaign like fishing bait to test your instincts and catch bigger, better keyword combinations. Review the reports to see what shoppers were searching for when matched to your bids. Draw more or better keywords from that data. (See the case study at the end of this chapter for examples.)

Tip: Check your categories.

When you're selecting ad keywords, plug them into an Amazon search. The top five subcategories that appear under "Show results for" are the most relevant. (See screenshot.) If your product is not listed within one of those five, your ad is unlikely to be displayed, regardless of your bid.

Move to manual campaigns and establish bids based on target metrics.

Once you've identified some keywords that work, create manual campaigns with those keywords and variations of them, perhaps starting with bids on broad matches and phrase matches.

Keyword variations are very important for phrase-match and exact-match types, and you can expect to add variations throughout the life of the product. Initially, the automated campaign will provide the bulk of variations and long-tail keywords, but eventually the broad-match and phrase-match words in your manual campaign will become a better resource for variations. (That's because by then, you'll have more search data for your specific product than Amazon, which can only pick keywords for your automated campaign from those in your listing and category — not everything users actually use to search.) You may wish to continue the automated campaign for a while, even as you begin a manual campaign, to continue harvesting keywords. At some point, the automated campaign will stop finding additional variations, and then you can retire the automated campaign for good.

Some sellers include top competitors' brand names in their advertising keywords. As noted in the section on identifying product keywords, we don't recommend this and Amazon considers it a policy violation. A shopper who enters the brand name has pretty good idea of what they want, so you're fighting an uphill battle to get them to click, let alone buy. For advertising, the ACOS is probably not worth it, and neither is an account suspension.

For all of your keywords, base your bids on data, not the unreliable information Amazon provides to suggest what a winning bid might be.

- If your product already has some organic sales, take the Detailed Page Sales and Traffic Report and look up your unit session percentage, which is essentially the conversion rate once a shopper has viewed your product page. If your keywords are reasonably valid, this organic conversion rate should be fairly close to your ad's conversion rate. Use that rate and do the math to identify a maximum bid that will achieve your target ACOS (and acceptable profit margin). Of course, the tools available can speed that calculation.

Sessions	Session Percentage	Page Views	Page Views Percentage	Buy Box Percentage	Units Ordered
28,309	12.17%	38,583	12.97%	100%	4,067
40,430	17.37%	52,074	17.51%	100%	10,113
5,393	2.32%	7,089	2.38%	100%	1,264
7,553	3.25%	9,327	3.14%	100%	1,288
4,457	1.92%	5,689	1.91%	100%	1,215

Units Ordered - B2B	Unit Session Percentage	Unit Session Percentage - B2B	Ordered Product Sales	Ordered Product Sales - B2B	Total Order Items	Total Order Items - B2B
706	14.37%	2.49%	$385,908.73	$66,781.78	3,229	457
370	25.01%	0.92%	$140,963.95	$5,049.10	9,180	195
267	23.44%	4.95%	$50,396.29	$10,566.14	776	120
222	17.05%	2.94%	$63,112.00	$10,878.00	817	98
193	27.26%	4.33%	$18,097.94	$2,819.04	706	87

Unit session percentage indicates the product page's conversion rate.

- If you're building visibility for a new product without many organic sales, you won't have enough unit session data to be as certain about your keywords or the right bids. Experiment, and expect to spend more time on the campaign than for an established product until you have better data.

Open your bids on the high end of your acceptable ACOS. As long as you outbid the next highest bidder, you may not pay your full bid per click anyhow. But note that you can bid well above Amazon's suggested high bid and still not get ad placement because conversion rates and maximum spend are also factors.

You can also bid the minimum of only two cents but still have your ad shown, if Amazon is impressed by your conversion rate and/or if all your competitors for that keyword have met their maximum spends, possibly by paying too much for other keywords that don't have a high probability of converting.

In the middle of that bidding spectrum are lots of sellers with products that convert moderately well and who will pay quite a bit for an ad. Position yourself on the low-cost end of that range, paying relatively little but with such a strong likelihood of a sale that Amazon will show your ad.

How do you locate that sweet spot? Experiment.

Run small, controlled tests.
Bid on a limited number of keywords for short periods. Keep close tabs on impression and conversion rates and ACOS to determine whether each $1 spent yields $100 in sales — or zero.

Top keywords in a category may get three or four times the impressions of a lesser keyword. What matters most, though, is sales. Identify which keywords get you sales and at what ACOS. Depending on your goals, you might be temporarily okay with a high ACOS or even a loss to get the flywheel going. On a great new product, this strategy could give it dominance in organic searches for that keyword so you could make up for lost profit in the future. But you can't advertise away your margin indefinitely.

Tip: Set up negative keywords, too.
Don't forget to include negative keywords in your campaigns. Protect your conversion rate (and make the entire campaign more effective) by ensuring that people who are clearly not after your product won't be shown your ad by mistake.

Get tools that ensure you can use your results data.
Amazon provides gallons more data about your keyword performance
than Google does. You'll receive weekly reports with perhaps 100,000
rows of data about what people are using to search and whether they're
buying.

You can drown in that much data without good tools to help you act on
it. The ideal tool summarizes the data to actionable steps, ranks
keyword quality, and alerts you to those you should do something
about. By distilling the myriad choices into a few big levers to pull,
you'll dodge the time-suck associated with keyword ad tweaking.

In fact, this might be the most important tool you can use, because
without a good tool to support proactive campaign management, you
can spend money on ads that don't help as much as they should.
Consider this "before and after" data from an ad campaign for a single
product. The top chart captures data from a combination of automatic
and manual campaigns that were set and ignored. It shows that, while
the advertising increased sales, it had little effect on overall session
percentage (conversion rate) or, more importantly, organic sales. Total
sales and ad sales are nearly identical. That's an indicator that the
campaign wasn't affecting search relevance as much as it should,
which in turn meant that the keywords in the campaign weren't ideal.

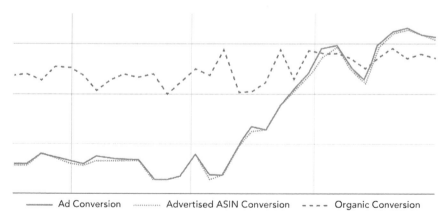

On the other hand, when the campaign was adjusted and managed
based on the suggestions in this chapter, including reducing bids on

ineffective keywords and increase phrase and exact-match bids, organic sales grew significantly, as shown below. This was because the ad click-throughs and sales increased the product's relevance for those effective keywords, so it also began ranking more highly in organic searches for those keywords, and that higher search placement prompted more organic sales, too. That's the flywheel effect, with paid clicks increasing relevance and search placement for organic searches.

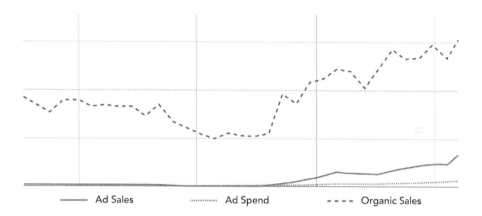

| —— Ad Sales | ·········· Ad Spend | - - - - Organic Sales |

Increasingly focus on long-tail keyword combinations.
Once you've started to identify successful keywords, focus your advertising spend. This doesn't necessarily mean higher bids on bigger keywords.

For any product, some keywords are more likely to lead to a sale than others — and some are better for Sponsored Products advertising. Counter-intuitively, these two groups are not identical, because the keywords most likely to result in a sale may also be the most expensive, so advertising on a weaker keyword can be a better investment.

True, a lot of people search using broad, high-level keywords like "bicycle" or "T-shirt." The problem is that many sellers are competing for those keywords, so they're costly, and your chances of winning the bidding is small. When you do, your ad may be seen by more shoppers, but a rather small subset might actually want your specific product. On the other hand, narrower, "long tail" keywords are much more available while also potentially more targeted to your ideal buyer. (Plus, as noted earlier, amazing numbers of people perform unique searches with those long tail terms. As a result, being the winning bidder on more small and inexpensive keywords is potentially far more effective than winning a very few big keywords.)

So instead of a broad keyword like "laptop," bid for "laptop touchscreen 8 GB RAM." The ad will cost less and the shopper will be more likely to buy because she already knows exactly what she wants. That means the feedback loop of "ad shown > shopper click > sale" becomes self-reinforcing, boosting your product's relevance in organic searches on those terms, too.

Continually expand your keyword selection and variations with new keywords that are narrow but still relevant. Fewer people will use them to search, but they're both less costly and more likely to lead to conversions. Pause the campaign as needed to make adjustments, and keep records to guide future campaigns. There are so many variables, including changes in Amazon's algorithms, that the "right" keywords will continually shift, so don't expect to stick with even good keywords forever. Be prepared to manage them continuously.

How many keywords per campaign?
Once you begin using exact-match bidding, the need to include multiple combinations of even a few words — like "best women's raincoat" and "raincoat women's best" makes the keywords add up fast, sometimes to several hundred or more. A campaign of 30 keywords would be fairly small. Regardless, adjust them as the campaign runs to make it as effective as possible. Sellers should expect to add variations throughout the lifespan of the campaign (and the product, if, like most, it needs an occasional boost from advertising).

Increasingly add exact matches to your campaign.
It's useful to begin campaigns (or add new, experimental keywords) with phrase matching and use the resulting reports to identify the actual search combinations shoppers use most frequently. But for any given keyword, exact-match bids will beat phrase and broad-match bids every time. So as you identify your most effective keywords, increasingly add exact-match bids on the most effective combinations.

Exact-match bids are the most restrictive, but they're also likely to attract your most targeted customers, for the same reason as narrower keyword combinations. That's good for conversion rates, and in turn more impressions and better organic search placement. Exact-match keywords may also be less expensive because there's less competition for them.

The three bid types
Suppose you're bidding on a keyword combination of "bottled alkaline water." You've got three choices for bidding:

- Exact-match bids for the entire keyword combo. The shopper must type "bottled alkaline water," **fully and in that order, no more and no less**, for your bid keyword to match.
- Phrase-match bids. In this case, the shopper could type "six-pack bottled alkaline water" and your product would still be suggested. Plurals are usually overlooked, along with additional words on the front or back, so "six-pack bottled alkaline waters" would match your keyword, too. But the search terms still have to be in **the same order as your combo, and other words can't be inserted between them**. "Alkaline water bottled" would not match, and neither would "bottled six-pack alkaline water."
- Broad-match bids, which in addition to singulars or plurals, **allows words to be reversed, omitted, or added**, and admits both some spelling variety and **synonyms**. Using the example above, the shopper could type "spring water,

---

alkaline," or any of the non-matching phrases above, and your product might still be suggested.[26]

Adjust your ad spend to meet your ACOS targets.
Once the campaign has run for at least two weeks, lower your bids on any keywords that get impressions but don't convert very well (and thus incur a higher ACOS than expected). Then any subsequent impressions and sales will better meet your ACOS targets. If that doesn't work, remove those weaker keywords.

---

[26] Sources for these distinctions: http://tinyurl.com/zgvvo4b and
http://www.salesbacker.com/blog/65/Broad__Phrase__or_Exact_Match__Which_Amazon_PP
C_Search_Type_Should_I_Use_

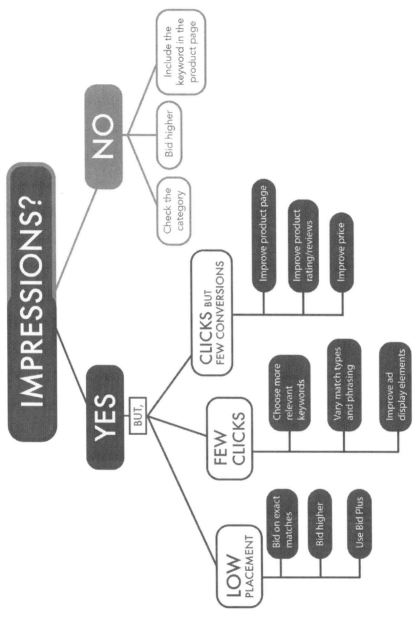

Start with automated campaigns to gain insight and keywords, then move to manual campaigns you can tweak as more data comes in.

If you're not getting many impressions for a keyword, assess whether it's simply not a great match for your product or your bid is too low. You can find out for sure by bidding significantly higher. If more impressions result, there's your answer—though you'll still need to decide if it's worth the ACOS.

If you want to spend less in general, remove broader keywords, which may convert well but probably at higher costs. When you want to spend more, increase the bids for your strongest keywords — especially those that result in a low ACOS. Or add new (and preferably narrow) keywords.

Bidding more — or more widely?

It can be hard to decide when to increase bids and when to add keywords. Amazon will tell you what a winning bid would be, but this amount is probably an average (and not the only factor in the system's ad placement decisions), so sellers often have to bid well above that amount to actually win good placement.

If you bid a little below that theoretical winning bid, particularly if your product has been converting well, you'll still receive impressions — sometimes plenty of them — just not as many as the winner. That's one case in which you might want to increase your bid slightly to see how ACOS changes. If you're still struggling to win impressions, however, you may need to bid much higher to get them. Only experimentation can prove whether the ACOS is worth it.

In 2016 Amazon introduced "Bid Plus," in which a seller gives permission to spend 1.5 times the bid to get top positioning on the results page. It's impossible to win that top spot without it. Using Bid Plus and tracking the results can be another way to determine if an increased base bid can put you among the frontrunners to make the increase worthwhile. If your bid is a long way from the winner, it's generally more effective to add keywords instead. See the troubleshooting section of this guide for more information.

Use your ad data to tweak the product listing.
Remove weak keywords from your most important keyword sources, the title and product bullets. Make sure those sources include your strongest keywords prominently. Add new, long-tail keywords to your hidden keyword lists to leverage your ad campaigns and further improve your organic search results.

Use the data to direct other marketing.
Take your successful keywords to other marketing channels.

Sponsored Products isn't your only Amazon option. There are others, some of which compete for the same space on search pages. For instance, the options of Amazon Marketing Services — headline search ads, product display ads, and a brand page — can be useful, but as of this writing, those campaigns can only be manipulated by hand and offer more limited results data. So gain confidence about your keywords, the conversion power of your product page, and how to design successful ads before taking that step.

Another option is Amazon Business. This B2B version of the marketplace is a low-overhead solution for buyers whose volumes warrant a discount or other special arrangements but aren't large enough to buy directly from you. (See the inventory management chapter of this guide for more details.) The keywords that work well on Amazon Business may be different than for the regular marketplace, but experience and data from one can inform the other.

All of these special programs can help drive traffic to your product and bolster conversions, which then improves your discoverability everywhere. As you get your product pages, keywords, reviews, and Sponsored Products ads working well, check out other promotional options to boost your flywheel momentum.

Similarly, when you've identified low ACOS keywords, advertise with the same keywords on Google, Facebook, or any other online channel.

Sponsored Ads case study

The best way to learn how — and why — to put together a Sponsored Products ad campaign is by walking through a real case. Take Plugable's Thunderbolt 3 display adaptor, for instance, which represented a new product category for the seller. Here's how the product manager got sales rolling.

Step 1: Discover keywords with an automated campaign. The product manager created an automated campaign with a strong initial bid but a conservative daily budget to ensure impressions without overspending on keywords that might not convert. After a week or so of sales (the timing depends on the product's sales rate), the product manager ran a search term report (the Automatic Targeting Report) to establish baseline costs per click (CPC) and better understand how customers searched for the product, including variations and long-tail keywords. That enabled him to identify the keywords that converted best.

Step 2: Increase control with a manual campaign. The product manager used those results to create a manual campaign with phrase and exact matching as well as broad matching. "Manual campaigns are superior to auto campaigns in many ways," he says. "The amount of granular control they give is one of the keys to success with Amazon Sponsored Products advertising."

He found that "thunderbolt 3 dual displayport" was a popular search in the automated campaign, so he used that keyword in the manual campaign. He added logical variations, including "thunderbolt 3 displayport," "dual displayport adapter," and "thunderbolt to dual displayport graphics adapter," to ensure exact matches with customer searches similar to the original keyword. These variations were important for capturing impressions using phrase and exact-match bids, and each keyword was added to the campaign under each match type (broad, phrase, and exact).

He continued the automated campaign for a while, too, to make sure he wasn't missing useful keywords.

Step 3: Ongoing refinement. As the campaign matured, the product manager treated it as a ongoing project: He reviewed the results regularly and continued to add exact matches for keyword variations. He also reduced bids on keywords that were underperforming (that is, resulted in low conversions and/or a high ACOS) — but he didn't eliminate them. He reserved the drastic step of pausing ads for a few keywords that were added in error or proved to be less relevant, with very poor conversion. For keywords with high conversions and low ACOS, he increased the bids to win more of those highly effective impressions. Finally, he continued to use the resulting search term reports to find great long-tail keywords to add to the campaign as exact matches.

Efficient Era

Chapter 5 —
How to Use Product Feedback to Drive Sales

In this section:

- Three reasons to closely manage your product reviews
- How to prevent negative reviews
- How to encourage positive reviews
- How to jumpstart positive reviews for new products
- How to capitalize on positive reviews
- How to handle and mitigate negative reviews
- Why smart tools are indispensable

Did we mention that the world has changed?
In the Wild West of e-commerce, where sellers and buyers move into and out of the market with fluidity and there's very little competitive memory (or loyalty to a brand or specific seller), the one thing that sticks around is product reviews.

A megaphone in every home?
If the Internet has changed anything, it's that personal opinions can be shared farther and wider than ever. It's not even that we all have a megaphone; we all have the equivalent of our own television stations. So word of mouth has more potential impact on sales than in the old days, when the opinions of ordinary consumers rarely reached the ears of more than a handful of people.

As a result, product reviews by ordinary buyers — and their placement at the point of sale —are key to today's sales model. Use this key to unlock sales.

Quality and service:
"Western consumers care about quality and customer service, and that is something most of China has not figured out yet." —Sam Boyd, successful private labeling support entrepreneur in China[27]

"You get what you pay for" means more online.
E-commerce also flips that statement on its head for the seller: You get paid for what you deliver. If your product is better, it can rise to the top.

In brick-and-mortar stores, consumers rely largely on brand recognition (read: big marketing budgets). Unless they're willing to invest time in research, they have relatively little insight about the product's performance in use to choose from sometimes bewildering options. So they're more likely to buy on price alone. (Just ask Wal-Mart.) That's inspired countless sprints to the bottom.

Especially for businesses that provide products with subtleties, what's great about online marketplaces is that product reviews make it easier to monetize quality and service. For sellers, they create incentives to offer better products. For customers, they go far beyond the information that'll fit on the package or even the relatively spacious product detail page. They alert potential buyers to how well the product works in the field, holds up over time, and compares to other brands.

---

[27] Boyd, Sam. Guided Imports,
http://www.reddit.com/r/Entrepreneur/comments/4br0z8/roughly_2_years_after_creating_a_c
ompany_in_china/

How e-commerce rewards quality

Plugable Technologies consciously chooses to work with manufacturers who charge a bit more because they deliver electronics products with higher quality than other suppliers (and therefore some of Plugable's competitors). One result of this strategic choice: I decided not to sell our products through a particular electronics box store, even though we do have traditional retail outlets.

Why diss the box store? The value of a quality premium breaks down there because there's no feedback loop among customers. That retailer wouldn't accept complete junk because it would create a returns issue for them. Particularly in electronics, however, the products at most physical stores are at or near the bottom of the range for feature sets, support — and therefore price. When customers stand before the shelf, they see two brands of the same product, side by side, with little to no unbiased or third-party information about the quality of either product or the incremental value of our higher-priced brand. Customers who've done their homework still might buy ours, based on details on the package, for instance, but a lot of customers haven't. As a result, they're less likely to choose it.

Enter product reviews: In our e-commerce distribution chains including Amazon, we get rewarded for our products' higher quality. Customers who do buy them have a better experience with them. They post more positive reviews than people who've bought our competitors' products. Those reviews guide the customers who haven't done other research. On Amazon specifically, that review edge translates into higher sales than our competitors enjoy. You can leverage that kind of review edge, too, whether your differentiators are product quality, product features, or service and support.

—Bernie Thompson, Founder, Plugable Technologies

Three reasons to closely manage reviews

In the e-commerce world, everything you do, from fulfillment to customer service to marketing activities, must cultivate positive reviews and mitigate negative feedback, both about the product and you as a seller.

But Amazon provides no resources to help sellers track product reviews, and even if you spend all day lurking on your product pages, you can't reach out to customers who leave new reviews without posting a public comment. Respectful public comments can be useful if the customer has said something that may confuse others and the information in your answer can help everyone, but generally, it's better to take on any issues as part of your support process instead.

Know when reviews are posted...

So one of the first tools you need when you enter an online marketplace is something to tell you immediately when a customer leaves a question or product review. By posting to your product page, customers not only leave direct feedback but also may provide valuable hints about their engagement with your listing at various points of the purchase process. To take their feedback seriously and use it to increase your success, invest in tools that alert you when customers leave you direct or indirect feedback, whether in the form of questions, refund requests, seller reviews, or product reviews. Note that these types of feedback typically, though not always, follow a predictable sequence or pattern as shown in the diagram below.

Why should you invest in feedback tools? There are several reasons:

1. To treat negative reviews as a customer service request. Don't shrug off bad reviews; they're a call to action. Even if you can't make things better for the reviewer, you can make a change that will ensure nobody else has the same bad experience, so future sales suffer minimally and the flywheel isn't dragged to a halt.

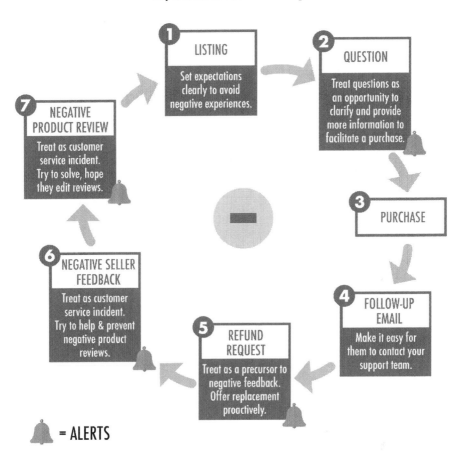

= ALERTS

The sooner you solve a customer's problem, the sooner you prevent negative feedback from accumulating and prompting more bad reviews in a Negative Feedback Loop.

2. To guide product offerings and development. When you can hear directly from customers what they like and don't like about a product — without the cost and difficulties of focus groups or other research — you gain critical information for product development and decisions about future growth. In addition, reviews can help you think outside the box about product features or markets, since customers may use your product in unusual ways or suggest ways to improve it that would never have occurred to you. This information is priceless for planning and future growth.

> # 86% of customers
> say they'll pay more for a better experience.[28]

3. To help drive the e-commerce flywheel. Reviews are one lever for the Amazon flywheel. They can help prod its motion or drag it to a halt. They're not as important to search rankings as sales, but they do factor in, and they certainly affect conversions. New products in particular will go nowhere without positive reviews.

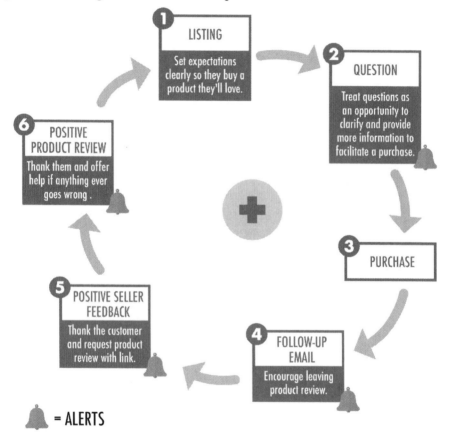

Encouraging positive reviews at every stage helps encourage purchases by others, initiating a Positive Feedback Loop.

---

[28] Oracle, 2011 *Customer Service Impact Report: Getting to the Heart of the Consumer and Brand Relationship*, http://www.oracle.com/us/products/applications/cust-exp-impact-report-epss-1560493.pdf

Quality, not quantity

Advice flies around the Internet — you must reach 10 reviews, or 50, or 100. But remember, for the Amazon flywheel, it's **sales** that drive search result placement the most. Positive reviews contribute somewhat, but generally reviews have more braking power than driving power.

In other words, a lack of reviews — or too many bad ones — can prevent sales more readily than good reviews can boost you in the search results. Nor is it true on Amazon that "a bad review is better than none."

So use your time wisely. When it comes to reviews, think quality, not quantity.

How to prevent negative reviews

Odds are that your product will find some detractors, but the ability to identify every customer can help prevent negative reviews. How? By making you quicker on your feet if you *do* run into a problem with your product — due to a supplier slip or raw material change, for instance.

In most retail experiences, if a customer has a problem, she has to send the item back and have the maker look at it before any replacement is sent. This is partly to ensure that the product is faulty, of course, and not merely beaten into failure with a hammer. But it's also because otherwise, the maker would have no way of knowing that this particular customer possessed the item at all. Clever fraudsters have built lifestyles on less.

There's no need for that step in e-commerce.

1. Ship exactly what you promise.

This may seem obvious, but it bears pointing out. Customers subtract stars for products that aren't quite what they expected, even if the difference is only cosmetic and they keep the product rather than returning it. Make sure product descriptions and photos are excruciatingly accurate. Update both when raw materials, features, color options, or other characteristics, including packaging, change.

Good automation tools can make routine catalogue maintenance less painful.

2. Ship *when* you promise.
Customers irritated by delivery delays may be negative about the product, too. Ensure that, whether you're using FBA or FBM, inventory levels ensure smooth fulfillment.

If you're fulfilling yourself, keep the customer informed with a shipping confirmation that includes the shipment method and, when available, tracking information.

3. If shoppers ask questions about your product, answer them.
The Q&A section of product pages is growing in use. The prominence of this section suggests that Amazon thinks that, like reviews, they're important, and there's evidence that products with answered questions rank more highly in searches than products with similar pricing and review ratings and volumes.[29]

---

[29] Mitchell, Will. "How to Rank Your Products on Amazon," http://startupbros.com/rank-amazon/

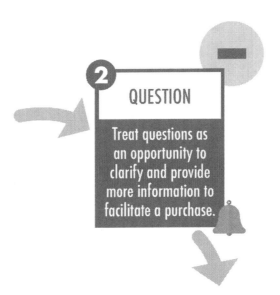

Unfortunately, Amazon notifications about new questions are unreliable. Set up a process for checking periodically for unanswered or incorrectly answered questions, or get an automation tool that will check for you. Then address them. Since other shoppers are likely to have the same question, prompt, helpful answers can turn into multiple sales. Ignoring them is likely to either prevent a sale or, if the sale happens, the customer may ultimately not get what they want and resent you for not helping them decide.

Once you've answered a question, revise your product description to incorporate the answer and make it easy for future shoppers to find.

4. Send replacements immediately. Don't wait for returns.

Once a customer contacts you for support (or you see other evidence of a problem), send a replacement immediately. Doing so can forestall a one-star product review. You already know that customer bought the product because you can trace the support request directly to the order through the marketplace email system. So make that customer happy *now*, before she has time to stew over a sluggish or reluctant returns process.

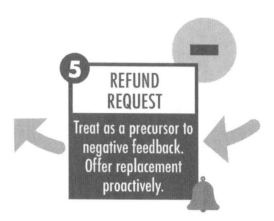

REFUND REQUEST

Treat as a precursor to negative feedback. Offer replacement proactively.

In some cases, a quick replacement might solve the customer's problem, so no refund request will be necessary. But even if the second unit doesn't do the job needed, sending it can forestall a one-star product review or net you a few more stars for effort.

5. Jump on refund requests.
If the problem gets as far as a refund request, that's a big red alert: You have a customer who's already taken one action and is warning you that another — a negative review — might be coming. (For fear of retaliation, most consumers wait until they have the refund in hand before posting a negative review.) Jump through that small window of time to try to fix the problem before that review hits.

Often, there may not be much you can do. Many sellers find that more than half of refund requests (for products that were shipped) are caused by goofs such as ordering the wrong thing. Still, make the attempt. The customer may just need coaching to set up or use a product he thought was defective. In such cases, a fast and appropriate response can save a customer relationship and either soften any negative review or prevent it completely.

This is particularly important for new products that don't have many reviews yet; in that case, and if the request is because the customer feels the product is faulty, it may even be worth sending the customer another unit right away to see if the second try is more successful.

6. Stay cheerful and helpful.

The griping on Amazon seller forums might lead you to believe that many refunds are demanded by problem customers who have a vendetta or keep a good product and want money back, too. In fact, the vast majority of Amazon refunds are related to *inventory availability and accuracy.*[30] Yep — odds are, it's your fault. So when you get a refund request, provide it quickly and cheerfully to forestall a one-star reaction.

7. Monitor for hijackers.

You probably know that your company doesn't own the marketplace listing you created, but a lesser-known ramification is that another seller can buy your product — possibly from you at bulk discounts — and sell it via your listing page. Arbitrage traders do this legitimately, but more shadowy characters can force themselves onto the scene as a variation of your product and sell it at a lower price. They take advantage of your positive reviews and search ranking while potentially damaging your business.

So keep an eye on your product pages for "other sellers." If a hijacking happens, contact Seller Support. (And see the troubleshooting section of this guide.)

How to encourage positive reviews

Cultivating positive reviews is crucial to overcoming the cold-start problem and igniting sales. Unfortunately, it's recently become harder to get a product's first reviews. Not long ago, sellers could distribute discount coupons to prompt purchases, and the resulting "incentivized" reviews were valuable even with disclaimers and without the "Amazon verified purchase" tag. In October 2016, however, Amazon completely banned incentivized reviews, other than those through its own Vine program. So unless and until Vine program

---

[30] Amazon: http://tinyurl.com/ncwwo7g

participation is extended to third-party sellers, it's become even trickier to kickstart reviews.

There are still steps you can take, and we'll get to those shortly. But make no mistake —reviews are a result, not a goal in themselves.

1. Keep the cart behind the horse.
Focus on satisfying customers, and good reviews will follow.

That doesn't mean you can shrug your shoulders and ignore reviews. Take the remaining steps to cultivate good reviews, especially for a new product, and do what you can to prevent or mitigate bad ones.

2. Know and follow the rules.
Remember that reviews exist solely to help customers make the right purchase decisions. They're not a thinly disguised promotional channel or a way to sneak in extra keywords.
Amazon is quite specific that, "Customer Reviews… aren't to be used as a promotional tool."[31]

Enforcement of the rules isn't perfect, but in the last year, Amazon has both tightened the rules and made it more difficult to game the system. Yet there's no need to join the black-hats. Create satisfied customers, and Step 3 will be easy.

3. Cultivate positive reviews with customized order and shipment confirmations.
"Cultivating reviews" may sound like manipulation, and it can be, if you go about it in the wrong ways. But if you're really trying to satisfy the customer, it's not manipulation; it's good customer service. Positive feedback is the natural result, and that feedback can be encouraged without violating Amazon terms of service.

---

[31] Amazon: http://tinyurl.com/zjqh4ro

Use each order's SKU information to send a customized order confirmation and ask for a product review. Take a look at the model below. Then scale this process with automation tools, including email templates for each of your products.

Sample order confirmation

Thanks for your order of:

• 6 Acme DooDads
• 1 Extra Large DooDad Holder.

Your order will ship no later than [date].

Once your DooDads arrive, you'll find complete assembly instructions inside the box. We don't expect you to have any trouble at all, but we're happy to help if you do. Save this email and reply to ask questions of our expert online support team.

Product reviews really help other shoppers, who also like hearing how people use our DooDads. Once you've had a chance to try yours, please share your experience at http://www.amazon.com/review/create-review?asin=XXXXXXXXX. We really appreciate it, and we know other shoppers do, too.

Thanks again for your purchase!

Joe Acme
Acme Customer Service Manager

Unsubscribe: We send just one email to confirm every order. Reply "unsubscribe" to opt out of these emails now and for future Acme orders.

4. Localize requests for better relationships and more reviews.

If you're going to take on the investment and risk of developing and marketing a product, don't leave a reachable chunk of the world market on the table. That's the advantage of digital marketplaces. But don't expect to develop great customer relationships — or earn the favor of a positive review — without speaking their languages. Literally.

当製品をご使用になりましたら、もしよろしければご感想をお聞かせください。弊社はお客様からのフィードバックを、弊社製品の今後の品質向上に活かしてまいりたいと考えております。

もしもお時間があるようでしたら、アマゾン・ジャパン様へ製品レビューをお寄せいただければ大変ありがたく思います。

Or perhaps we should say, *Voudriez-vous nous donnez votre avis?*

When asking for reviews, use the languages each customer understands best. That means creating separate email templates for every major geography into which you sell, based on either the marketplace or the shipping address. We've all groaned at laughable or incoherent translations in the instructions for imported products; don't earn the same disdain.

Paying attention to localization issues is a key part of being really successful everywhere. Cultural sensitivity counts. The example email above might be too casual for a Japanese customer, for instance. But a great advantage of the U.S. melting pot is that we have resources everywhere to help with such concerns. Tap into them through your workforce, the suppliers of your automated tools, or online.

5. Don't overlook non-marketplace buyers.
Sure, reviews that are "Amazon Verified Purchases" may carry somewhat more weight than reviews by non-Amazon customers, but many shoppers don't look past the average star rating.

So ask customers who buy your product from your web store or other channels to post an Amazon review, too. Add the request to order confirmations, shipping notifications, and any other positive communication with customers. Make it easy by providing a link.

6. Err toward polite, not pushy.
Provide useful information or help first, and make the request a distant second. Keep it conversational. Remember, you're asking for a favor, so try not to ask more than once. And honor the relationship — if customers ask to unsubscribe, unsubscribe them. Blacklisting tools can help to ensure you don't alienate otherwise loyal customers by re-subscribing them every time they order.

How to jumpstart positive reviews for new products
New products and new listings are subject to one of those cold-start Catch 22s: For reviews to be posted, someone has to acquire the product, but most shoppers won't buy a product without any reviews. They probably won't even know about it, since the existence of reviews factors into search results; your new product may be buried behind thousands.

Don't assume the Vine program can help you, at least for now.
Now that Vine is the only legitimate way to incentivize reviews, many sellers are ready to sign up for Vendor Express (or accept an Amazon invitation to become a Vendor) so they can take part in Vine. We don't recommend this, and not only because the Vine fees are substantial. The real trouble is that vendors hand most of the control of their businesses — from the product listing to pricing—

---

to Amazon. There may be sellers for whom this is attractive, but for most, simply turning into a supplier for Amazon is too steep a price. For now, we can only hope Amazon opens Vine up to third-party sellers on other terms.

So generating initial positive reviews that give a compelling and accurate view of the product, while following policies, can be tricky. A combination of advanced techniques can help:

1. Make sure existing customers know about your new product launches.

You can't buy reviews or provide any other compensation, but you can encourage customers who buy the product to leave a review, and your current customer base might be more likely to take a chance on your new product before it has any reviews. It's against policy to send marketing communications to customers within the Amazon system, but that's why you should always be building your own customer list — so you can use it to let them know you have a new product and extend those relationships.

2. Consider associating the new product with a well-reviewed variation.

Can your new offering legitimately be related to another of your products as a variation on fundamentally similar products? If so — assuming the existing product has good reviews — you can associate the new variation through the variation fields on the Amazon product page backend. These include size, scent, color, and a size/color combination.

Don't overlook a variation possibility. Think broadly about how those options might be defined. The size variation might encompass an electronics product with more ports or plugs, for instance, or two winter apparel products that are functionally and cosmetically the same but with different insulating values. Similarly, you can use the scent variation to reflect a variation that has less to do with the nose than with something else customers would legitimately view as a version of the same thing but that doesn't have its own category of variations.

Use variations in good faith. If you have the customer's best interests at heart, variations allow you to help everyone by associating a product the customer might prefer with another well-reviewed product you sell.

Less scrupulous sellers may group a number of minimally related products — including new and untested products — to take advantage of one well-reviewed product. Sometimes the variations aren't at all like the product reviewed. Such strategies don't typically succeed for long, however, since negative reviews generally follow. Make sure that from the customer's perspective, an associated product is as good and as proven as the one that's reviewed.

Monitor any automatic associations. Amazon may associate products for you, though they might get it wrong — or hurt more than they help. For any automatic associations, make sure negative reviews remain stuck with the "old" product that prompted it — not newer products with better reviews.

3. Participate in Amazon's Early Reviewer program (if and when you can).

If no product variation applies to your situation, consider participation in the new Early Reviewer program. Still in beta testing and only available to a few sellers at the time of this writing, this program is intended to help new products get those first crucial reviews.[32] There's no indicator of that participation to customers. Those who buy an eligible product may randomly be prompted by Amazon to leave a review; the incentive is a gift card for a nominal amount (typically a couple of dollars). The gift card can be used on a future purchase, but since the participant has already paid full price for the product in question, and purchased it without knowledge of the incentive, there's no conscious or unconscious motivation to leave anything but an

---

[32] Amazon: http://tinyurl.com/hhn9zjw

honest review. They're still flagged on the product page with an "Early Reviewer" notification.

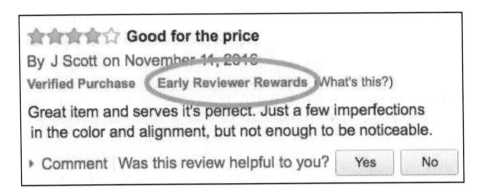

Of course, the Early Reviewer program does nothing to raise the search results ranking or visibility of a new product prior to those first sales, when the need is greatest. And it's still in flux; it remains to be seen whether sellers will be able to elect participation, or wait for an invitation, or if Amazon will simply identify products without any reviews on its own. But ultimately it could be useful, so keep tabs on its development.

How to capitalize on positive reviews

Get a good one? Pat yourself on the back. But don't stop there. Remember the Plan/Do/Check/Act cycle mentioned in the Introduction? Reading reviews is a check stage. Don't neglect to also act:

1. Check your inventory levels.

Particularly for new products, a spurt of positive reviews can kick-start the flywheel. Unnoticed success can kill a product if it sells so quickly it goes out of stock. Make sure your growing momentum can't be lost.

2. Listen to the customer voice.

Customers can be a deep well of ideas for promotion, new feature or options, and new applications. Analyze good reviews, looking not only for comments like, "I love it. Wish it also came in blue" — but also less obvious insights about potential accessories, crossover markets, new sizes, etc. Identify new keywords based on words happy customers use to describe the product. Document those gems to feed new product and business development.

3. Give recognition where it's due.

Happy customers can help motivate employees. Use excerpts from or accumulations of positive reviews to recognize and even reward successful product teams.

> **More than 80%**
> of employees are motivated by appreciation.[33]

---

[33] Brooks, Chad. "Appreciation Motivates Employees to Work Harder, Study Says," *Huffington Post*, Nov. 19, 2013, www.huffingtonpost.com/2013/11/19/appreciation-employees-work-harder-motivation_n_4302593.html; and Dabawala, Kamal. "Appreciation: A Powerful Tool for Employee Motivation," http://www.academia.edu/4802498/Appreciation_A_powerful_tool_for_Employee_Motivatio n

Studies show that appreciation from their bosses is one of the key things that motivates workers; positive feedback from customers can be your entrée.

How to handle and mitigate negative reviews

Despite your best efforts, a few negative reviews are likely to slip in. But nobody *wants* to have a crummy experience! Most negative feedback is really a request for help.

Unfortunately, Amazon doesn't make easy to treat it as such; you have to make an effort to hear that cry for help, tease out which order prompted it, and respond. This does qualify as a grey area from the standpoint of Amazon policies, but it's also the only way to do the best possible thing for the customer — even if that means pointing them to another product that might meet their needs better.

So here's how to save the customer relationship, or at least prevent the damage from spreading.

1. Pay attention.

It's crucial to be aware of negative reviews immediately, and not only to manage your brand reputation. Depending on situation, the review might be your first notification of a real problem with a supplier, product batch, or inventory stock. Read closely, match the review with a buyer, and respond accordingly to make sure it's not the first review of many to complain about the same problem.

The need for good tools

Amazon provides little seller support related to product reviews, because you are not who the reviews are intended to serve. The only way Amazon provides for you to find out about new reviews is by browsing your product pages, and the only way to respond is with a public comment. To be competitive, additional tools are crucial. The right tools for matching buyers with reviews can alert you to new reviews, arm you with the details you need to respond, and even automate appropriate responses.

2. Don't stress if it isn't the start of a trend.

Depending on the type of product, many shoppers put more stock in an average star rating that includes a few negative reviews — in these cynical times, it helps validate that reviews are real and not rigged. And after all, nobody likes everything equally. If you doubt that, check the one-star reviews for award-winning movies, acknowledged classic books, and other bestselling products.

That said, you shouldn't ignore a crummy review.

3. If the customer's problem can be fixed, fix it.

Online sellers can give better service than in most retail experiences; take advantage of that opportunity. If you get a negative review that could be fixed by a product replacement, act. Treat it like a call for help and feed it into your customer service or support system.

4. Respond directly and follow up with public comments if it might help others.

Many customers will update reviews if you've been able to help them, sometimes even just for making the effort. Whether the customer ever changes the original review or not, if it contains inaccurate information, you can always go back to it and post a public comment along the lines of "Glad we could help you by phone" so that others see that you do follow up. It's important never to dismiss the reviewer or their concern, but when appropriate, you can phrase your comment in a way that subtly points out the correct information for future readers.

79% of customers
who share complaints online are ignored by the companies they're complaining about. Stand out by responding. The payoff? More than half of those who get responses feel better about the brand, and **almost one quarter post a more favorable comment**.[34] Even if these ratios don't translate directly to product reviews or seller ratings, they indicate how much goodwill can be saved by a simple response.

Why smart tools are indispensable

There's no way to respond to a negative review quickly enough without smart tools, because you've only got minutes, not days or weeks. But with the right buyer-review matching tools, you can act promptly. Link the review to an order, contact the customer, and offer

---

[34] Oracle, 2011 *Customer Service Impact Report: Getting to the Heart of the Cosumer and Brand Relationship*, http://www.oracle.com/us/products/applications/cust-exp-impact-report-epss-1560493.pdf

a replacement or refund. As when a customer contacts you with a problem, send the solution without waiting for a return. Act quickly and cheerfully enough, and you might convince the customer to change his review.

Some experts advise asking for the review to be changed. It's not a good use of time, it may be perceived as pressure, and if you take care of them correctly as soon as you spot the problem, they'll likely change the review on their own. Even if they don't, you've helped salvage a relationship and prevented the customer from spreading the ill will any farther.

Tool Description: Review Notifications with Buyer-Reviewer Matching

Efficient Era offers just the tool you need for tracking reviews. We will alert you every time you receive a new product review or seller feedback so you can act quickly. Under normal circumstances, your actions are limited, especially when it comes to negative reviews. Fortunately, Efficient Era's Buyer-Review Matching Tool automatically matches Verified Purchase reviews to their order number, so you can communicate directly with the buyer and thank them for kind words — or solve any problems they have.

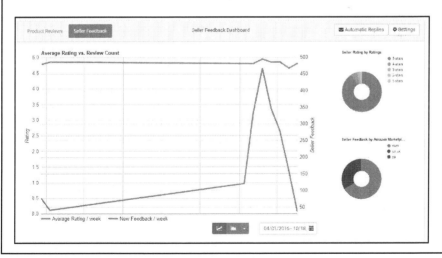

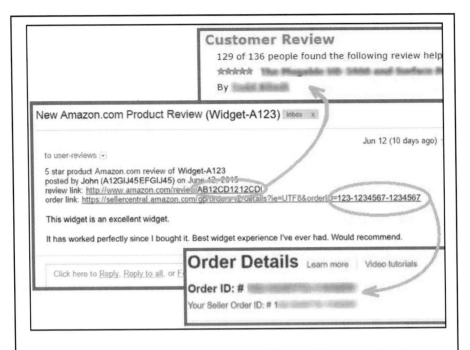

"This is by far the best service for matching customer review to Amazon orders — nothing else that we have used even comes close." — Devin K.

Chapter 6 —
How to Be Popular: Managing Seller Feedback

In this section:

- Why you should care about seller feedback
- How to ensure great seller feedback
- How to turn lemons into lemonade
- How to use positive seller feedback to increase sales
- What smart automation tools can do for you

The customer wants to buy — but do they want to buy from **you**?

Customers are as aware as you are that everyone and his dog can be an Amazon seller, and that means the company they're about to give hard-earned cash to is as likely to be a clever teenager on a far continent as a Fortune 50 company. If a potential customer hasn't dealt with you before, she at least wants to know what others think.

Why you should care about seller feedback
Product reviews easily have ten times more impact on your product's success or failure than seller feedback. But great seller ratings can reassure nervous buyers and help make sure first-time customers come back.

Perhaps more important, seller feedback is a precursor. A customer who takes the time to provide seller feedback is more likely to post a product review, too. If you manage seller feedback closely, you're likely to increase both the quantity and quality of your product reviews.

---

10 – 20% of sales:
Amazon says that most sellers receive seller feedback on 10 to 20% of their sales. Track your own percentage and aim for the upper end of that range — or more. Then look at what that feedback implies.[35]

Happy customers may silently smile. Unhappy customers shout. Research demonstrated long ago that customers who don't get good service are likely to tell many more people than happy customers are. How much more likely? 2 to 1, 10 to 1, some other multiple? Estimates vary for how much louder unhappy customers can be.[36] But the exact ratio doesn't matter. What matters is that if you're not creating reasons for your customers to smile — clear information, quick deliveries, snappy responses to questions — they might turn and bite you instead. Seller feedback is one of the first ways customers can smile — or bite.

Faster than same-day delivery
Providing feedback on a seller is faster than a product review — a few clicks and a word. As a result, seller feedback may be posted before the customer has even received the product. So make sure your early interactions with the customer prompt them to see plenty of stars.

Time does not heal all. Complaints don't fade as fast today as they used to. The one-star rating in your Seller Ranking will be there

---

[35] Amazon, "Why Don't I Have More Feedback?" Feedback FAQs, http://tinyurl.com/hkw3n8w

[36] The defunct White House Office of Consumer Affairs is widely cited, but other research supports the point. See http://www.linkedin.com/pulse/20130604134550-284615-15-statistics-that-should-change-the-business-world-but-haven-t and http://www.assetbasedmarketing.com/marketing-news/myth-the-average-unhappy-customer-will-tell-10-people-about-the-poor-service-he-or-she-received.html

indefinitely, tugging down your average. Even a so-so rating of 3 stars — a passing "C" grade in school —is subtracted from your percentage of positive ratings. Aim for As.

Who cares? The search engine. Who even looks at seller feedback, compared to the star of the show, product feedback? True, most potential customers only see your overall rating. Few people take the time to click through the comments. But seller feedback *is* a factor in search result ranking. Delight customers with great service, and you'll help ensure future customers can find your product at all.

	30 days	90 days	12 months	Lifetime
Positive	93%	91%	92%	93%
Neutral	2%	4%	3%	3%
Negative	5%	5%	5%	5%
Count	562	1,189	4,248	12,564

It's no coincidence that this seller wasn't the buy box holder. They may be risking an account suspension if much else goes wrong.

Who cares? Amazon. Amazon's performance targets suggest that no more than 5 percent of seller feedback be negative or neutral, and negative feedback is counted in your Order Defect Rate and Seller Rating.[37] And of course, top sellers earn ratings much closer to 100 percent positive, so the risk of account suspensions for low ratings is almost beside the point. If you expect to compete, keep 5 percent negative well in the rearview mirror.

Remember, too, that unhappy customers are more likely to take the time to rate you. Amazon's account pages almost encourage any uneasy customers to do so, since anyone checking on a delivery

---

[37] Amazon, Customer Metrics, http://tinyurl.com/hk8evnm and Introducing Amazon Seller Rating, http://tinyurl.com/zdfbmk4

promise can hit the Seller Feedback button from there. So an unhappy contingent rather smaller than 5 percent of your customers can put you over that 5 percent misery threshold. The result could be a seller account review.

Tip: Prevent a devastating account suspension.
Seller ratings can be a factor if anything goes wrong and the customer involves Amazon in fixing it. Regardless of your seller performance metrics (order defect rate, pre-fulfillment cancel rate, and late shipment rate), sellers with weaker customer metrics may find their accounts suspended while Amazon figures out what's going on. Make sure your seller rating earns you the benefit of the doubt so your account stays active in the meantime.[38]

More metrics focus on service. Amazon's overall seller performance metrics include several elements related to service. These include metrics that incorporate data about customer contact and return response times. Seller feedback is one of your first warnings that something's gone amiss. Take it as your first opportunity to intervene in a relationship headed south.

How to ensure great seller feedback

The obvious answer — if more easily said than done — is to respond quickly to orders and messages, ship promptly (when you're not using FBA), and get it right. In particular:

1. Watch for customer emails daily.

This includes Saturday and Sunday. Weekends count, both to customers and for Amazon's customer response time metric. If you don't want to work 365 days a year, get a tool that will automatically alert you, and when feasible, respond.

---

[38] Amazon: http://tinyurl.com/ncwwo7g

Tool Description: Seller Feedback Automation Tool

Unfortunately, Amazon does not email you when you receive seller feedback, good or bad. Efficient Era's Seller Feedback tool provides email notifications, dashboard-based analytics of your seller performance, and the ability to automate emails in response to each instance of positive or negative seller feedback.

---

2. Answer customer messages promptly.

This is critical, whether the message comes before or after an order or as a reply to a message from you. Amazon research indicates that answering messages within 24 hours ensures 50 percent less negative feedback compared to taking more than 24 hours.[39] Auto-responses don't count.

3. Verify that you're not overlooking customer messages.

Review the response time report available at the bottom of the Buyer-Seller Contact Response Time table in your Seller Central customer metrics.

4. When acknowledging orders, create a personal connection.

A follow-up email is an opportunity to create a relationship with the customer, particularly if you can customize it to the product and the season, for instance. (Good tools such as a selection of templates and automated email customization can help.)

---

[39] Amazon: "Contact Response Time Metrics," http://tinyurl.com/gng9ftr

Tool Description: Email Automation Tool

With Efficient Era's Email Automation Tool, you can set up follow-up email campaigns that get triggered based on events such when the order was placed, shipped, or delivered, including any delays you specify. Weave placeholders into your message to dynamically address the buyer by name, refer to the product they bought, and even add a link to the product review page. Format with our rich text editor or modify the HTML code.

5. Demonstrate your commitment to service.
Let the customer know how to contact you if they have any questions or trouble. Surveys show that many of your competitors are working hard to improve service these days; you need to do so just to keep up.

43% of businesses
with fewer than 500 employees are focusing on improved customer experience as a growth strategy.[40]

---

[40] Wasp Barcode Technologies. *2016 State of Small Business Report,*
http://www.waspbarcode.com/small-business-report

6. Once you've established a connection, ask for feedback.
Before you end that confirmation email, ask the customer to let you know if your service is up to snuff. Include directions or a link. Pleased customers may give you good seller feedback before the product even ships simply because you've demonstrated that you care about them.

7. Consider your return policies and processes carefully.
Crowd-pleasing sellers authorize returns automatically when the request is in line with Amazon's timeframes. Speed counts. Additional generosity in the return period can also reduce the likelihood of negative seller feedback. The dollar value of protecting your seller rating—and therefore search placements and Buy Box share—can far exceed the cost of a few returns.

If you still get negative feedback, mitigate it by responding well.

How to turn lemons into lemonade
The data Amazon provides about seller feedback isn't very actionable, and it's even harder to respond quickly and efficiently. You can't spend all day hunched over your Seller Central dashboard.

But don't simply grit your teeth at a bad rating. Make the best of a bad situation—or turn it around completely—with these steps:

1. Keep blame where it's due.
Make sure Amazon strikes seller feedback that's really about FBA service. (This correction is increasingly automated.) That's one of the key advantages of FBA versus FBM status — Amazon takes responsibility for prompt shipment. When they're at fault for lousy fulfillment, that rating will be eliminated from your average. The rating itself and any comments won't disappear, but they will be lined out with a note that the problem wasn't your fault.

2. Don't ignore other negative feedback.
The right tools can identify which order, for which product(s), generated a given piece of seller feedback. With that information in

hand, you can quickly determine the best action and distribute responsibility for responding to the appropriate members of your team.

3. Learn from the help they're giving you.

The information in negative feedback is incredibly valuable, as anyone familiar with continuous improvement management philosophies knows. A customer who leaves you that kind of gift is teaching you how to get better. Accept that help. Analyze both positive and negative feedback to drive improvement processes and business management decisions, including how you manage order intake, inventory, customer service, and fulfillment processes and teams. Doing so will not only prevent the same problem from annoying another customer, it might help you gain an efficiency advantage over competitors.

In particular, Amazon notes that the vast majority of refunds that move through its system are caused by problems with *inventory availability and accuracy* — not quality issues, sizing difficulties, or customers who changed their minds.[41] So eliminate listing, inventory, and fulfillment glitches to leap ahead of many competitors.

---

3 (or more) to 1:

It's at least three times, and as much as 10 or 20 times, easier and cheaper to sell again to an existing customer than to find and convert a new one.[42] Do your utmost to use negative feedback to prevent chasing off any more.

---

4. Use the chance to prevent a bad product review.

Keep in mind that seller feedback is an early warning system. A customer who provides negative seller feedback is more likely to post a product review, too — and they're already cranky.

---

[41] http://tinyurl.com/ncwwo7g

[42] The *Harvard Business Review* references that some industries might have as much as a 25 to 1 ratio: http://hbr.org/2014/10/the-value-of-keeping-the-right-customers/

Besides, when you read negative product reviews, you'll sometimes see customers complaining not about the product per se, but the service — damage in shipment, missing instructions, or a product that's not what was pictured or described.

Suppose you're selling thousands of units and getting 20 or even 50 seller ratings for every product review, because they're so much easier, because Amazon asks for seller ratings, and because a customer checking on an order can do it readily from her account page. Those bad seller ratings are a valuable warning that negative product reviews might be in your future. Listen!

Treat a negative seller rating like a sick canary in a coal mine. You've got a narrow window in which you might be able to correct the problem and ensure that more visible feedback — the product review — is good.

5. Feed negative seller ratings into a customer support process. That support can be manual or an automated trouble ticket. What's important is that you quickly reach out to that customer with courtesy and sympathy. Try to help them resolve their frustration. At worst, you'll look attentive. You may improve their mood enough to prevent a bad product review. At best, they may revise or remove their seller feedback, too.

86% of customers:
Global research by Genesys, a provider of customer service systems, has shown that, across cultures, well over three quarters of customers welcome proactive contacts if it appears they might need help.[43] Negative feedback is nothing if not a cry for help. Reach out to that customer to improve their long-term opinion of you.

Believe it or not: Fast is better than helpful. Recent research by a Nielsen-McKinsey joint venture indicated that twice as many customers appreciate a quick but not-very-helpful customer service response over a slow but more effective response.[44] This is probably because a speedy contact helps the customer feels heard and important, even if the person who contacts them can't do much but apologize.

That doesn't mean a sloppy, rude, or inaccurate response is okay. Fast *and* effective still wins. But the research results show how important speed is to consumers. Get going.

How fast is fast? Respond within 24 hours of negative feedback. That's the timeframe customer service research has found to be acceptable, and which Amazon expects you to meet when responding to messages from customers.[45] (Your success in doing so is incorporated into your Seller Rating.)

Amazon is pushing hard to shrink that 24-hour expectation, though. The new seller metric related to customer contact response time sets a

---

[43] Genesys. *The Cost of Poor Customer Service: The Economic Impact of the Customer Experience and Engagement in 16 Key Economies.* 2009.
http://www.slideshare.net/fred.zimny/the-cost-of-poor-customer-service-the-economic-impact-of-customer-experience-in-the-us
[44] NM Incite. *The State of Social Customer Service, 2012.* Still available at www.slideshare.net/NMIncite/state-of-social-customer-service-2012, among others
[45] BenchMarkPortal. *Email Customer Service in Small and Medium Sized Businesses,* 2005.

12-hour response as the performance target by the fourth quarter of 2016.[46] It won't be long before customers get used to that norm.

So unless you have nothing better to do than keep a browser trained on your seller feedback page — weekends and holidays, too — create or pay for a system that alerts you to the negative feedback, correlates it to an order, and sends a response.

An email that does these things effectively might look like this:

Poor seller rating? Here's an appropriate email response.

We're so sorry our service after you ordered a Wonder Company Electronic Widget wasn't what you expected. We'd love to make it right.

If you'd like to contact our expert customer support team, you can reach us at [800 number and/or email]. They'll be quickest if you have your order number, **123-4567890**, handy.

We do appreciate your purchase and strive to give excellent service, too. We hope you'll give us another chance to please you.

Suzanne Wonder
CEO, Wonder Company

Unsubscribe: Reply "unsubscribe" to opt out of these emails now and for future Wonder orders.

---

6. Don't ask for a negative rating to be removed or modified.
Some e-commerce advisors suggest that, when you reach out to the customer, you also ask for a better rating. The problem is that customers may feel like that's all you care about — not them. In that case, you're poking a wound. If they feel as though you're trying to silence them, they may get even louder on social media.

---

[46] "Amazon's New Performance Metrics…," 888 Lots, Dec. 22, 2015, http://888lots.com/blog/expert-advice-amazons-new-performance-metrics-other-recent-changes-and-how-to-minimize-your-suspension-risk/

So avoid the temptation to blow the tentative goodwill you may have generated by reaching out. (Besides, Amazon policy prohibits pressuring a buyer to remove feedback, with "pressuring" left undefined.) Focus on making the customer feel better, and the reviews — and any removals of bad ones — will take care of themselves.

7. Consider creating a blacklist of customers who've left negative feedback.

The idea is not to create a dartboard for your wall or to refuse orders from these customers but to avoid prompting them for feedback in the future. You know they're cranky, toward you or in general. So it's not in your interest to encourage them to leave future feedback. If they choose to, that's their business, and you can respond accordingly.

Similarly, you may find that repeat or regular customers don't need as many emails from you—order confirmations, review requests, feedback follow-up, etc. — as a new customer. You don't want to sour that strong relationship with spam.

So coordinate your order intake and follow-up process with appropriate databases or tools that manage who should receive various types of follow up.

Tool Description: Review Notifications

Efficient Era offers just the tool you need for tracking seller feedback. We will alert you every time you receive new feedback, and we match the feedback to an order, so you can act quickly to respond to any rating that is less than stellar. That way, you can communicate directly with the buyer to try to solve the problem they had. And if they're beyond help, you can avoid poking the bear by not asking for their feedback next time.

---

8. Track your rating as a key performance indicator (KPI).

If your seller rating is anything under 100 percent and doesn't improve over time, you're not handling that feedback correctly. Make a change.

In a competitive marketplace where plenty of sellers earn 100 percent positive ratings, you can't afford to underperform them for long.

140% more sales:

A recent study quantified just how worthwhile it is to give customers a good purchase experience. Those who have the best experiences spend 140% more over a year, compared to those who have the poorest experiences, regardless of the product type or purchase frequency.[47]

Make sure your service is up to par to transform it from a perceived cost center to a sales driver.

If you follow these steps and improve shaky processes, negative ratings should fall off over time. Then *all* of your seller feedback can help you increase sales.

How to use positive seller feedback to increase sales

All your seller feedback is positive? Great! Make it work harder for you.

1. Watch for new feedback and identify who left it.

Again, simple tools can do this for you, correlating the feedback to the order. More sophisticated tools can automate additional steps, too.

2. Show your appreciation for positive ratings.

Email the customer (through the Amazon system, as permitted) and thank them for the kind words. It doesn't hurt to suggest they contact you with any questions or eventual issues. This is a simple step toward a long-term relationship.

---

[47] *Harvard Business Review*, "The Value of Customer Experience, Quantified," August 2014, http://hbr.org/2014/08/the-value-of-customer-experience-quantified. Original report at http://www.medallia.com/resource/revenue-impact-great-customer-experience/

> **Who?**
> One difficulty with online marketplaces is that customers may overlook your name and remember only that they bought on Amazon. Help satisfied customers remember your company for next time.

3. Turn positive seller feedback into positive product reviews.
While you're thanking the customer, ask for a product review, too. Don't beg for stars or, for heaven's sake, suggest reviews using particular keywords or other information. Nobody likes to be bossed around, and it's definitely against the spirit of Amazon rules. Make sure none of your great reviews disappear in a periodic Amazon purge because someone suspects you of nefarious practices.

Simply ask the customer to help future shoppers by sharing details about their use of the product. Make it easy by including a link to the item's Amazon product page. Technically Amazon doesn't permit links in emails, but it's hard for them to object to sending the customer back to an Amazon page.

Tailor a short, sweet email that does these things effectively, using the model below for ideas:

Sample thank you and product review prompt

Thanks so much for the kind feedback on this order!

If you ever have any trouble at all, we're here to help! Just reply to this email reach us.

And if you're using the product regularly: It's a big help to us and other customers to hear what you most appreciate about our product, what problem it's solving for you, and how it went.

You can submit your product review here:
[ReviewLink]

Thanks again for taking the time to write about your experience!

Bea Success
Stuff, Inc.

Unsubscribe: Reply "unsubscribe" to opt out of these emails now and for future Stuff orders.

---

4. Don't push products, accessories, or anything else.

Remember that Amazon puts strict limits on marketing through their order email system. Besides, customers have low tolerance for spam. The last thing you want is for a customer to *lower* a good supplier rating. Offer help, not hype.

5. If a customer engages with you, respond again.

If your email receives any reply but "unsubscribe," send another response. Since the customer has initiated that additional interaction, it's only reasonable to reply, even if it's not a specific question or issue.

Don't jeopardize customer satisfaction, and its potential impact on your seller performance metrics, by failing to respond to any message that needs answering. And if no response is needed — if the customer simply replies "Thank you," to an order confirmation, for instance — don't forget to indicate this to Amazon within 24 hours of receipt.

What smart automation tools can do for you

Of course, successful sellers get dozens, if not hundreds, of seller reviews a day. Responding can definitely help expand that success, but at those volumes, manual processes won't cut it. Get help.

1. Make the flood of reviews manageable.

Smart tools and templates can do nearly all of the work for you:

- Alerts
- Order matchup
- Service ticket integration
- Email templates and customization
- Automated email within 24 hours

2. Help build a loyal customer base.

In retail sales for relatively big-ticket items, you might find out who the customer is through a product registration system — but more likely, you won't. (Product registration systems rarely capture more than a quarter of customers.)[48]

With online sales, you know exactly which customer bought which product and when, even for an item that only costs a few dollars and doesn't have a built-in motivation for registration.

Being able to reach each customer is important. Research has shown that building business with existing customers conserves marketing

---

[48] http://www.ns.umich.edu/new/releases/23102-product-registration-companies-should-make-it-automatic ; also http://www.dmnews.com/digital-marketing/boost-value-of-product-registration/article/71231/, http://www.marketingsherpa.com/article/how-to/4-tactics-to-lift-product, http://m-ize.com/resources/best-practices/increase-product-registration-rates/

dollars and increases profits.[49] The impacts vary by industry, of course, but unless you're selling a pure commodity, building customer recognition of and loyalty to your brand is likely to pay off.

65% vs. 10%
The average probability of making a sale with a current customer compared to selling to a new customer.[50]

The right tools can tell you if a given sale is to a repeat customer and which of your products they've purchased before. Use that information to provide better support — and help keep that customer coming back. The goal? Customers so happy, they'll write letters like this:

A real customer letter to aim for (with names changed)

Dear Wonder Company Representative,

I'm so impressed with Wonder Company. I've been using the Wonder Widget for a couple years and suddenly it seemed to start acting up. I troubleshot the issue with your Sammy Support, who I must say is an excellent reflection upon your company...always friendly, knowledgeable, and helpful. You can almost feel the smile in his helpful email replies. He made me feel like your most important customer! ...[A]fter exhausting all options, Sammy did a most generous thing; he gave me a one time complementary new unit...unbelievable service! I mean, I was way out of warranty but he just wanted to solve my problem.

It's extremely rare these days to experience truly world-class customer service. I was a phone support tech for ATT for 6 years. They constantly updated us on what was the latest in world-class customer service. I'm proud to tell you that Sammy embodies that ideal. I'm proud to tell you that Sammy embodies that ideal. I will certainly spread the word about your product and company.

---

[49] For example: Gallo, Amy, "The Value of Keeping the Right Customers," *Harvard Business Review*, Oct. 29, 2014, http://hbr.org/2014/10/the-value-of-keeping-the-right-customers/; Jao, Jerry, "Customer Retention Should Outweigh Customer Acquisition," *CMO*, Aug. 2, 2013, http://www.cmo.com/articles/2013/7/18/customer_retention.html
[50] Marketing Metrics data as reported in http://www.momentology.com/7286-loyalty-marketing-strategy-experts/

I'm a busy guy and don't write a lot of these kinds of letters, so I hope you can know that I am truly impressed with your operation. If Sammy exemplifies your staff, Wonder Company should expect to keep on growing, as your customers can't be anything but satisfied...I know I am!

Yours truly,
Garrett Gomez, a proud customer

Chapter 7 —
How to Manage Inventory and Fulfillment to Keep the Flywheel Humming

In this section:

- How to make smart fulfillment decisions
- How to manage stock to keep the flywheel turning
- How to capitalize on bulk orders

It's as simple as this: Going out of stock stops the flywheel dead. Avoid it at all costs. Unfortunately, in the weeds of inventory management, managing stock can be anything but simple.

How to make smart fulfillment decisions
When you first joined the Amazon marketplace, one of your first decisions was probably whether to fulfill yourself (fulfillment by merchant or FBM), to have Amazon handle fulfillment (fulfillment by Amazon or FBA), or to use some combination of both. Revisit that decision occasionally as your business grows and your product mix and related Amazon fees change.

1. Start with FBA, especially for new products.
For most products, it's a simple decision to choose Fulfillment by Amazon (FBA), at least initially. FBA is a top reason for many sellers' success.

First, the search engine favors FBA products, which are also eligible for Amazon Prime. So especially for new sellers or products, there's almost no way to spin the flywheel fast enough without FBA.

> # 27% of Amazon sellers
> ## use FBA exclusively.[51]

The Amazon search engine focuses heavily on conversion rates, so you want all your rates to be as favorable as possible from Day One. Plugable, which uses both fulfillment methods, waited to launch a recent new product until it was in-stock at Amazon, with the thought that it's better to explode out of the gate than trickle out of it — which might've been the case if the product had been launched as FBM first. The company doesn't have conclusive numbers to justify that strategy, but it does know that FBM products don't rank as highly in searches, and therefore sales likely wouldn't have built as quickly as they did.

Another advantage, of course, is that letting Amazon handle fulfillment allows you to focus your resources on better management and growth instead of logistics. Finally, surveys indicate that, although it can be costly, FBA is more profitable for many sellers, perhaps because of the impact on volumes and thus economies of scale.

> # 27% higher profits
> ## are reported, on average, by FBA sellers than FBM sellers.[52]

Finally, with the exception of a new program called Merchant Fulfilled Prime, only FBA products are eligible for Amazon Prime. There's little doubt participation in Amazon Prime increases sales, since Prime members make purchase decisions based on the product eligibility for that free, two-day shipping.

---

[51] *The State of the Amazon Marketplace 2016*, Feedvisor and Web Retailer, http://fv.feedvisor.com/stateofamazon.html
[52] Ibid

> **63 million customers**
> are members of Amazon Prime. That's more than half of Amazon customers and more than half of U.S. households.[53]

You can participate in Merchant Fulfilled Prime regionally around your factory or warehouses, where you can guarantee that quick shipping to nearby delivery addresses. Otherwise, FBA competitors have an advantage. There are situations when FBA isn't the best answer, but it's the exception, not the rule.

2. Make thoughtful decisions about FBA inventory options.
When you set up your product listings, pay attention to inventory options and defaults. Specifically:

- If you're the manufacturer of record in the Amazon Brand Registry, consider the stickerless, commingled inventory option, which relies on your UPC or other unique product identifier. For those product categories that qualify, commingling can save you the expense and risks of manual labeling and make your overall global inventory easier to manage.
- Think twice — maybe more — about repackaging. The risk is that a returned product that's imperfect or incomplete will be shipped to a new customer and make them unhappy, too, potentially wreaking havoc with your seller performance. It's usually better to ensure that you get returns back so that you can inspect and deal with them.
- One option to consider instead of repackaging, in fact, is participation in the Certified Refurbished program. If you have returned goods sent back to you, you can verify that they're still like new (or make them so) and resell them without losing

---

[53] Shi, Audrey. "Amazon Prime Members Now Outnumber Non-Prime Customers," *Fortune*, July 11, 2016, http://fortune.com/2016/07/11/amazon-prime-customers/

sleep over what that second customer will find when they open your package.

- The inventory placement service may sound good if your volumes with Amazon are still small, since it allows you to consolidate shipments to one Amazon warehouse, but it can significantly delay inventory availability. The default, distributed inventory placement, gives you more control.

3. Revisit fulfillment decisions periodically.

FBA does have drawbacks, especially for large products such as furniture or appliances, particular categories, or very seasonal products that may incur substantial storage fees in their off-season. FBA inventory also sometimes gets lost, damaged, or misplaced, or otherwise requires a call to Seller Support. That's why many sellers use a strategy that combines FBM and FBA.

52% of sellers
use both FBA and FBM.[54]

When making decisions between FBA and FBM, consider these factors:

- Product category
- Product size
- Product margin
- Seasonality
- Total number of Amazon products
- Shipping cost efficiency
- Turn rates

Once upon a time, sellers could rely on Amazon for virtually all their storage needs, but many of the largest have since opened their own warehouses and handle some of their own fulfillment to avoid punitive

---

[54] *The State of the Amazon Marketplace 2016*, Feedvisor and Web Retailer, http://fv.feedvisor.com/stateofamazon.html

storage fees or stock limits. In most U.S. locations, warehouse space comes pretty cheaply.

$5.08 per square foot
is the average annual U.S. warehouse cost.[55]

---

4. Prepare product-specific contingency plans.

At times, Amazon can barely build warehouses quickly enough to keep up. As a result, they sometimes pass on their space constraints to sellers in the form of higher storage fees, inventory ceilings, or both. Be prepared to move or liquidate problematic inventory.

Involuntary fire sales

An Amazon seller one day received a notice from Amazon that, in a particular geography, the company could stock no more than 2,000 total units in Amazon's warehouse, regardless of the number of ASINs involved. "At the time, across all of our products, we already had more than that in stock, so we couldn't ship more units of a few products that were going out of stock," the seller recalls. "We had to hold 'fire sales' and give away some slower-moving stock to make room for those items that were selling quickly because we couldn't afford to let our bestsellers go out of stock, even briefly. If we had, they'd have lost their momentum and search placement and stopped being bestsellers at all."

Similarly, if Amazon switches your inventory from one warehouse to another, the transit and receiving time—which can vary between warehouses—can throw off the best plans. Nothing's more frustrating than suffering a stock-out and losing sales (and search ranking) when you know the product is sitting there on a pallet somewhere and just hasn't been processed. But there's nothing you can do but try to ensure that it's not *your* replenishment or shipping that causes the problem.

---

[55] Colliers International, *North American Industrial Market Outlook, Q4 2014*, http://ow.ly/KpBP0

When it comes to cash flow and inventory, you may already feel like you're sometimes on the edge, but expect to occasionally be pushed further. Prioritize your products and know your options for alternative storage, fulfillment, or liquidation.

> ### 30% of businesses
> with more than 100 employees consider cash flow among their top challenges. The percentage is as high as 39% for smaller businesses.[56]

How to manage stock to keep the flywheel turning: 10 best practices

Once your product is selling and being well reviewed, and as a result earning good placement in search results, the most important key to holding onto success is staying in stock. Having goods to sell is even more critical than a traditional retail environment.

Maybe you're a hard-core proponent of just-in-time inventory. Or perhaps you have idle warehouse space and take a more traditional view of your inventory investment. Either way, you know inventory is expensive. But for online marketplaces, going out of stock is even more costly.

In the old days, a stock-out might temporarily reduce service levels and make a retail partner unhappy, but it didn't affect future sales so much or so permanently as it does in an online marketplace today.

Stay in stock to maintain momentum. You've spent time and money to get your product noticed, convert sales, make customers happy, and generate positive reviews, and Amazon rewards you by moving the product up in search results. If you follow that effort by letting it go out of stock, you're not merely losing a sale or two. You're losing all the momentum you so carefully built. The flywheel stops, and your

---

[56] Wasp Barcode Technologies, *2016 State of Small Business Report*, http://www.waspbarcode.com/small-business-report

product falls to the bottom of the search list again, so that even once you have stock, shoppers won't be able to easily find it.

That causes big problems. Amazon uses some combination of the product's trailing daily, weekly, and monthly sales rates as the most important variable when assigning search results placement. But they don't weight the longer-term metrics heavily. Based on anecdotal experience, one day of zero stock is bad, but you can probably recover with a week or two. It might take a month to recover from a three-day stock-out. If you're out of stock for two weeks, you'll probably have to start over completely.

So how do you make sure you stay in stock? Follow 10 best practices:

1. Recognize the impact of stock-outs on sales.

Look at past sales volumes over time as they correlate to the product's inventory levels.

Then correlate sales and inventory with page views and events such as promotions or an influx of reviews to identify when stock-outs have been driven by unexpected sales. Use trend lines to get a sense of the lost sales (and even lost page views) that resulted.

By clarifying the consequences of a given stock-out on the long-term sales trend, and the resulting opportunity cost, you'll be better able to prioritize replenishment activities, determine appropriate order quantities and timing, and assess when a purchase risk might be worthwhile.

2. Use a planning horizon at least as long as your supply cycle.

For private-label sellers, staying in stock can be tricky. Amazon provides you an inventory summary and low-stock alerts through the seller dashboard, but they assume you either have a supply in your own warehouse or use a reasonably local (and prompt) supplier, so they only alert you a few weeks, at most, ahead of a stock-out. That's not nearly enough time for most private-label sellers. In addition, the alerts consider sales velocity in isolation from other factors — including seasonality, your advertising plans, and, most important, product reviews. As we've already discussed, reviews can have tremendous effects on sales, once magnified by the search results flywheel.

So think of Amazon's alerts as a fail-safe, not a trigger for reordering. Instead, understand your lead times and the factors that affect them, and plan replenishment proactively enough that you can all but ignore the low-stock alerts.

Tip: Forecast six months of sales.

When you place a PO for goods from Asia, the best-case scenario for manufacturing, shipping, customs, and Amazon receiving processes is probably a two-month turnaround. The worst-case scenario — for products with extensive customization or material supply difficulties — might be four months or more. So expect to predict sales as far out as six months.

Long Asian resupply cycles can mean a hit on accounts payable, too. Be prepared for that inventory investment. And protect your cash flow as much as you can by keeping all your products in stock. Track resupply times, and reorder based on the longest — not optimism, promises, or averages.

---

3. If you're sourcing from China, don't overlook Chinese New Year.
Factories that shut down for the better part of a month affect reorders substantially. Get a copy of Chinese New Year dates for the next several years, and remember that factories may shut down to begin celebrating days or even weeks before the actual date. Plus, in the weeks leading up to that, more factory clients than usual may be in order queues with you.

This issue is somewhat exacerbated by Amazon's decision to raise storage rates for November and December, the busiest months in the retail year, and reduce the rates for October. Although the company is offsetting the change by reducing weight-handling fees for items shipped in November and December, this rate structure encourages you to sell off inventory by year's end, rather than letting it carry over.[57] That helps to ensure you're not letting inventory languish, and it's fine if you're careful to have enough for December shipments, with inbound orders for early January, too. Do be certain that by December, amid the usual rush of holiday sales (by the Gregorian calendar), you're prepared to place additional orders for inventories you won't sell until February or later.

4. Manage every product individually.
Shun one-size-fits-all inventory planning and replenishment. Yeah, it's easier, and you can't ignore the greater efficiency of consolidated orders and shipments. But if you treat every product the same, you'll always run out of stock on the products that sell better than average. As a result, they'll stop selling at all.

So when it comes to replenishment, beware of batching. Read up on just-in-time inventory methods, tweak your processes to enable a reasonable facsimile of those ideals, and don't let your slow-movers hamstring your hits.

Tip: Be ready for the success of a #1 ranking.
It's useful to note that if you have a rising product, the increase in sales from a third place ranking to second or first typically isn't linear but exponential. That means when sales start going gangbusters, you've got to be prepared for ever-larger sales jumps. Anticipate carefully for inventory purposes and don't be shocked if you suddenly need a rush air-shipment. It's almost always worth it to keep that sales velocity screaming.

---

5. Monitor promotions to ensure they don't suck your inventory dry.
When you run a promotion with a coupon or discount code, pay attention. Promotions can be *too* successful, not only cutting into your margin more than expected but running your inventory to zero so that all the benefit of the promotion, from a search placement standpoint, is immediately lost, and you're worse off than you started.

---

[57] Gonzalez, Angel. "Third-Party Sellers Giving Amazon a Huge Boost," *The Seattle Times*, May 31, 2016, www.seattletimes.com/business/amazon/amazon-to-host-forum-for-its-marketplace-merchants/

Fortunately, you can take a couple of steps to control the quantities of any promotional sales. First, you can protect a portion of your existing inventory by creating a fulfillment order to yourself and then putting that order on hold for two weeks. That reserves the inventory without shipping it.

Then watch your sales carefully. When orders during the promotion reach a quantity that will soon threaten a stock-out, end the promotion. Then cancel the fulfillment order on hold, and that inventory will become active again.

You can avoid any potential delay by Amazon, which indicates that ending a promotion can sometimes take a few hours, by first editing the promotion to change the valid discount code. Any subsequent attempts to redeem the original code will fail. Depending on how you've communicated the promotion, you'll need to remove references to it or announce that it's over. This method assumes that your promotion wasn't positioned as fully valid until a certain date, but you can always phrase that as "Good until X date *or while promotional supplies last.*" That way, you shouldn't get complaints that the promotion has ended even though you still seem to have stock, and it may help add urgency to the promotion for those you're targeting.

6. Use the data available to improve your sales forecasting.
Dispense with crystal balls as much as you can. Amazon provides an overwhelming amount of data; use it.

You're likely already correlating sales with advertising and other promotional attention to decide where to focus your marketing budget. Don't stop there. Get comfortable estimating probabilities based on product reviews.

You know every product's sales velocity by geography, as well as its most recent reviews. New, positive customer reviews probably mean you'll sell more. Factor that probability into your purchasing decisions. To do so, keep a close eye on those reviews and average ratings. Look back on the historical impacts of well-regarded reviews to inform decisions.

On the other hand, if you have a product that's getting dumped on by customers, you don't need to worry about ordering more soon. Focus instead on product improvement.

7. Err on the side of too much supply.
Make sure you can accommodate a little extra supply, whether by budgeting emergency drayage or storage costs, arranging a supplier-managed inventory agreement, or reserving space in your own warehouse. As noted previously, U.S. warehouse space is inexpensive compared to losing Amazon sales momentum.

Avoid a quick road to bankruptcy.
There are plenty of stories about a product that took off after great reviews — and then the seller couldn't keep up. At best, these stories represent many lost sales. At worst, by the time the seller got large volumes into stock, the products had lost all momentum and quit selling. If cash flow is constrained, such a sudden sales spike is a quick road to bankruptcy. Be careful. Hold onto momentum.

You can't expect to predict natural disasters, but you can make sure three-day weekends, routine storms at sea, or a supplier's equipment breakdown don't cause a stock-out. A shipment that arrives 72 hours too late can cause nearly as much damage to flywheel momentum as one that's a week late. And a two-week delay is a disaster.

8. Use judgment to take risks for big successes.
Automate inventory decisions to the degree that's practical, but don't put them completely on autopilot. There will always be factors that require human intervention, including a jump in a product's star rating, the launch of a related product, or a particularly threatening new competitive product. Consider such events as you forecast and order.

For instance, if you're launching a product you really believe in and that has a substantial market, that's the place to take a risk. If you get even one or two good reviews, place a good-sized PO. That purchase won't be justified by prior sales, but sellers with runaway hits repeat that success with other new products by estimating sales based on their bestsellers, not more average performers.

Sure, such risks are stressful. Make a bad decision or overrate your own product, and you might break your company. But a decision that's bad because it's too conservative might kill a great product that would've otherwise *made* the company. Don't play it so safe you run out of stock just when the product takes off.

Stepping out of the data

"If we really believe in a new product, we step out of the data for it," says a seller with a string of best-selling products. "Because if we don't take that risk, our inventory will limit sales and therefore growth potential. Part of the reason one of our products has been the top-seller in its category for a solid two years is that, after our first early days, we've made sure it's never quite gone out of stock. As a result, it's never slipped out of the top search results." The flywheel is humming along, as it should.

"Of course, we've gotten that wrong a few times and ordered way too much," he adds. "We've also erred on the side of caution and run out of stock lots of times. But most of the time, taking a risk was the key to a big success. Otherwise we'd have run out of stock and the product would've died."

---

9. Diversify products to mitigate the risks.
Expect to make some mistakes. Just don't let any one error kill the company. No single bad decision should bankrupt you if you diversify your products and manage their replenishment individually. The less volatile products can provide a small safety net.

If it makes sense for your business, try to have a portfolio mix that includes products from fast-growing markets as well as mature ones.

Many businesses use the Boston Consulting Group Product Portfolio Matrix to organize their products into quadrants based on relative market share and market growth:

- **Cows** are products with a high relative market share in slow-growth markets. They bring in cash that can fund growth for other products.
- **Stars** have a high share of quickly growing markets, which makes them promising, but they often require a funding boost to increase market share.
- **Question marks** have a low share of fast-growing markets. Although the market is promising, the product's standing suggests that you need to evaluate it and either boost market share with promotion to put them into the Star category, or divest them as Dogs.
- **Dogs** have a low market share in slow-growth markets. They don't bring much money into your company, and they consume management time and money, so they ought to be gradually liquidated.

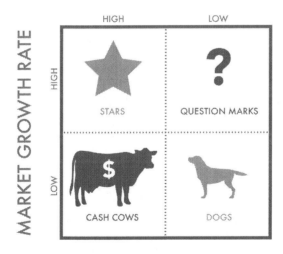

The Boston Consulting Group Product Portfolio Matrix can help you balance your product mix to enable risks when it makes sense.

10. Take advantage of inventory planning tools.

It's shocking, but nearly half of businesses with fewer than 500 employees track inventory manually or not at all.[58] Among Amazon sellers, the percentage of those doing it by hand is more than two thirds. Even those with more than $2.5 million in annual revenues aren't using tools wisely; barely half of those use inventory management software.[59]

In one stroke, implementing a system with even some automation can put you ahead of more than half of your competition.

68% of Amazon sellers
don't have inventory management software.[60]

Amazon provides plenty of stock and sales data as flat files, but without manipulation, it's hard to tease out the implications so you know how to act. But that raw sales data, when correlated with inventory and promotional events, becomes useful in a big way.

So create or buy good tools to help you make sense of volumes of data and turn it into easily visualized forms that drive decisions and actions. For each product, consider:

- How much shipped in the last week
- The maximum ship rate over time
- How much stock is currently available, both at Amazon and at your own warehouse, if you have one
- What inbound stock is expected, on what schedule
- How many weeks of stock exist as a result
- How the inventory levels are affected by advertising, promotions, or new great reviews

---

[58] Wasp Barcode Technologies, *2016 State of Small Business Report*, http://www.waspbarcode.com/small-business-report
[59] *The State of the Amazon Marketplace 2016*, Feedvisor and Web Retailer, http://fv.feedvisor.com/stateofamazon.html
[60] Ibid

Use that data to create projections and identify your own triggers for transferring stock or placing new orders.

How to capitalize on bulk orders

Depending on your products, there are a couple of ways to take advantage of the fact that not every order is one product at a time. The owners of many small and medium-sized businesses have realized that often Amazon offers prices that are as good as or better than their usual sources.

48% of B2B customers
already or will soon order at least half of their supplies online.[61]

Here's how to court more bulk orders:

1. Build special relationships with customers who place large orders.

As with a lot of things, Amazon will give you data about a large order if you know where to look (or have tools that will alert you). Pay attention. A bulk order can indicate a potential new market, or at least a customer who's worth a bit of special attention. Give more service "touch" to such buyers to ensure their orders are repeated.

You also might want to handle orders over a certain quantity threshold outside of your normal processes. For instance, tailor your order confirmations to include more direct service support or information about tax exemption documentation.

2. Run promotions specifically for businesses and other bulk-order buyers.

Through Seller Central, Amazon provides tools you can use to promote appropriate products to other businesses, as long as certain conditions are met. The available promotion types include discounts,

---

[61] *Internet Retailer, 2016 B2B E-Commerce 300*, http://www.internetretailer.com/b2b-ecommerce/#!/, as reported by Brook Software Solutions, http://insights.brook.ie/blog/13-statistics-highlighting-how-important-inventory-management-is-to-your-business

free shipping, and BOGO promotions. By setting purchase thresholds for your promotion, from minimum quantities to minimum spends, you can make the promotion apply only to bulk orders. For instance, you can create a "buy 10 get 2 free" promotion or a discount that only applies to a dozen units or more.

You can also use the advanced options in the "money off" promotion type to create bulk pricing tiers for all of your products, excluding any to which the tiers shouldn't apply.[62]

3. Promote your products to other businesses through external advertising.

Target business buyers with advertising placed outside of Amazon, such as in Google AdWords or Facebook, that drives shoppers to your Amazon listings. (Make sure your ad copy clearly indicates that it's a special offer for bulk orders so that shoppers who aren't your target audience don't click on it.) Not all advertising efforts outside of Amazon are successful, so be sure to test an ads on a small scale, for a limited time, before going all out. Finally, as previously noted, consider sending traffic to an intermediate landing page, such as a blog or Pinterest board. A lot of Facebook ads, in particular, are hit by clickbots and fake accounts with no real interest in your product, and you don't want them clicking directly to your Amazon page and affecting its sales conversion rate. Intermediate pages can defeat such nuisances, pre-qualify buyers, and send them quickly on to your Amazon listing for sales.

4. Identify products that might be appropriate for Amazon Business.

If you're getting many bulk orders, consider joining Amazon Business at http://www.amazon.com/business. This marketplace can be useful if your products are likely to appeal to buyers looking for tiered pricing, tax exemptions, purchase order referencing, or specific supplier certifications. The program fees are the same as for a Professional Selling Account, as is the FBA vs. FBM option.

Participation favors volume over margins, and the performance requirements are stricter, but tax exemption procedures are more

---

[62] Amazon: http://tinyurl.com/z8dmjpu

automated. Amazon Business participation may also be worthwhile if you can claim particular credentials, such as ISO 9001 or Forest Stewardship Council (FSC) certification, that drive decisions in your market and that would be easy to overlook in the regular Amazon product pages.

Since participation is monthly, you can try it for a few months to see if it's worth managing your listings and processes separately. Amazon recently introduced charts to help you track sales attributable to Amazon Business; some sellers find it represents 20 percent or more of their business and that a significant number of regular customers begin using that option when it's available.

Tool Description: Bulk Order Notification Tool

As important as bulk orders are, Amazon offers no way to know when you've received one. Checking manually is never the way to go, either — you want to be able to act quickly and not waste work-hours keeping an unending watch over your orders. With Efficient Era's bulk order notification tool, you define a bulk order threshold for each of your products, get notified immediately when you receive one, and can take appropriate action from there.

"I love the large order email from Efficient Era. I use this to keep an eye on my FBA inventory levels and also to help me see when I need to add a listing with larger quantities to give my customer a better value." —Kathy M.

Efficient Era

Chapter 8 —
How to Compete with the House and Still Win

In 2016, the number two concern for most online sellers was competition from Amazon itself. (Number one was losing their seller privileges.)

> **44% of sellers worry**
> about Amazon branding the products they sell.[63]

It's not a new problem. The AmazonBasics brand launched in 2009 with consumer electronics, but by then Amazon had been competing with other private brands for at least five years.[64,65] Those have grown to more than 3,000 products categories that range from kids' clothing to original streaming video to furniture.[66]

The problem for sellers is that Amazon knows your secrets. The company admittedly watches successful products, particularly those that bring in more than $100,000 in revenues a month, and digs into

---

[63] *The State of the Amazon Marketplace 2016*, Feedvisor and WebRetailer, http://fv.feedvisor.com/stateofamazon.html
[64] Amazon press release, Sept. 19, 2009, http://phx.corporate-ir.net/phoenix.zhtml?c=97664&p=irol-newsArticle&ID=1333481&highlight=
[65] Steiner, Ina. "Amazon.com Selling Goods Under Pinzon and Strathwood Private Labels," http://www.ecommercebytes.com/cab/abn/y09/m06/i03/s03
[66] "AmazonBasics House Brand Flatters Competitors, but They're Not Fans," *Seattle Times*, April 23, 2016, http://www.seattletimes.com/business/amazonbasics-house-brand-flatters-competitors-but-theyre-not-fans

their data to assess what makes those products work — from product features to keywords — before deciding to create its own copycat.[67,68] So the nearer your product is to being a bestseller, the bigger the target on your back.

In addition, there's good evidence that Amazon is tilting the table. For instance, Amazon branded products often appear in three or four categories, while the company is becoming more strict about allowing third-party sellers to list in just one. For products that are highly relevant in multiple categories, that's a significant disadvantage.

Still, third-party sales are more profitable for Amazon than its own, and the company is not likely to overlook that.[69] It's in Amazon's best interests to retain healthy third-party sellers, and smart private-label sellers can beat the odds to survive. Here are 10 ways to dodge the bullet:

1. Don't panic.
One company with a long-term bestselling product met its worst nightmare when Amazon launched a competing line using the same manufacturer. The bad news: The Amazon product quickly displaced the seller's meal ticket, reducing sales exponentially.

The good news, however, is that the seller hung in there at number two. That's still high enough for customers to find them, notice their great seller ratings, and consider the advantages of buying from an acclaimed service expert. Plus, anytime Amazon slips up and goes out of stock, the seller's product is poised to slip back into first place, at least temporarily.

---

[67] Cohen, Jeff. "When Product Liability Insurance Makes Sense for Your FBA Business," Seller Labs, May 11, 2016, http://www.sellerlabs.com/blog/when-product-liability-insurance-makes-sense-for-your-fba-business

[68] Clausell, Tristan."The Best Kept Secrets of Amazon's Private Labeling Initiative," Skubana, April 20, 2016, http://skubana.com/amazon-updates/the-best-kept-secrets-of-amazons-amazonbasics/

[69] Gonzalez, Angel. "Third Party Sellers Giving Amazon a Huge Boost," *Seattle Times*, May 31, 2016, http://www.seattletimes.com/business/amazon/amazon-to-host-forum-for-its-marketplace-merchants/

> **$131 billion in third-party sales**
> boosted Amazon's bottom line in 2015.[70] You can still get
> a respectable share: 70,000 third-party sellers exceeded
> $100,000 in sales.[71]

2. Address potential inventory impact.

When you move from a number two or number three position into the top spot, the sales increase is typically not linear but exponential. Unfortunately, the reverse is also true. So if the Amazon knocks you out of a bestselling position, you might see sales drop a lot.

Prevent the bad news from compounding by reacting immediately. Revisit your inventory management and purchasing so habitual replenishment processes don't keep placing orders until you're swimming in excess inventory, with its cash flow challenges.

3. Super-charge your service and support.

The Amazon brand carries an enormous advantage, but the brand comes with expectations that can work in your favor: Customers will expect a flawless experience, even more than they do from other sellers. And liberal refund policies and fast shipping aside, Amazon employees can't be experts in everything.

That gives smaller sellers two advantages:

- Lower expectations.
- The ability to provide better support.

So become the expert. Train your support staff to be experts, too. Know how your product is used in the real world, not just most commonly but across the spectrum of purchases. (That means studying customer reviews and talking to customers directly when you can.)

---

[70] Ibid

[71] "Amazon's Bezos: I Believe We Are the Best Place in the World to Fail." *Seattle Times*, April 5, 2016, www.seattletimes.com/business/amazon/amazons-bezos-i-believe-we-are-the-best-place-in-the-world-to-fail/

Generate and update product FAQs based on the questions prospective customers ask about compatibilities, integration, and cross-brand accessorizing. Update your product detail pages to preemptively answer those questions.

Over time, your seller rating will reflect how much better you are as a resource for current and potential customers. Sure, people will still buy the Amazon brand, but if your supplier and product ratings can keep you in the game, you can still succeed.

4. Learn from the master.
It's good to have a mentor. Study how Amazon describes and markets products similar to or identical to yours, and aim to be better.

Impossible? Not at all.

Fewer than 5% are bestsellers:
Most Amazon branded products aren't ranked number one.[72]

Many Amazon branded products shoot upward on release to grab the bestseller spot, but plenty don't. In fact, of more than 900 AmazonBasics products, one recent snapshot indicated that fewer than 5 percent were number 1 bestsellers. Heck, more than three quarters were not even in the top 25![73]

Those rankings are remarkably low, considering. They demonstrate that Amazon isn't taking advantage of its control of search placement.

They also reveal that rock-bottom prices are not the last word for shoppers. Given Amazon's buying power and willingness to employ loss leaders, it can probably do anything a competitor can at a landed price that's at least slightly lower. That means that for 95 percent of

---

[72] Clausell, Tristan. "The Best Kept Secrets of Amazon's Private Labeling Initiative," Skubana, April 20, 2016, http://skubana.com/amazon-updates/the-best-kept-secrets-of-amazons-amazonbasics/
[73] Ibid

AmazonBasics products, product quality, known brand names, and service still influence a lot of customer decisions.

> **50% of Amazon unit sales**
> were attributed to third-party sellers by late 2016 — and the rate continues to grow despite more Amazon branded products than ever.[74]

Put those factors to work for your products, and you're likely to beat Amazon's sales ranking. Focus on earning perfect seller feedback so search results display why the buyer should click to your product page even if you're not at the top of the list. Constantly drive your product pages to earn a higher conversion rate, finessing your keywords, product photos, and details and generating more five-star reviews to ensure that everyone who sees your product pages buys.

5. Create something better.
When an Amazon copycat displaces yours, turn up the volume on your product development team. Scour customer reviews and support contacts to fix quality weaknesses or develop a Product 2.0, 3.0, 4.0.

Imitation may be the most sincere form of flattery, but a copycat will always be a half-step behind. Stay ahead to avoid competing purely on price, a battle you're unlikely to win.

6. Focus growth on products where you have or can build an expertise.
Another lesson to take from Amazon: They're constantly expanding their product offerings — averaging more than 20 per month.[75] Grow your product portfolio, too.

---

[74] http://www.statista.com/statistics/259782/third-party-seller-share-of-amazon-platform/ and Rao, Leena. "This Lesser-Known Amazon Business Is Growing Fast." *Fortune*, Jan. 5, 2016, http://fortune.com/2016/01/05/amazon-sellers-holidays/
[75] Clausell, Tristan. "The Best Kept Secrets of Amazon's Private Labeling Initiative," Skubana, April 20, 2016, http://skubana.com/amazon-updates/the-best-kept-secrets-of-amazons-amazonbasics/

But be selective. As you expand, look most closely at products that require expertise, not those that anyone can import and slap a label on. The more complex your product, or the harder it is to support well, the more you as a small seller have a big opportunity to provide better support that Amazon can.

If Amazon creates its own version of your silicon spatula, you're in trouble. If they create a branded version of a product that bundles well with related products or has to interface with various mobile phone platforms or respond to software updates over time, for instance, you stand a much better chance of being able to offer customers superior information and support. As a result, you'll earn better ratings and the chance to keep your product selling.

7. Don't beat a dead horse.
Although Amazon adds copycat products rapidly, it also quickly retires those that don't take off.[76] This is another way to learn from a winner.

Periodically review your whole portfolio. Identify products on the low end of your bell curves for sales, star ratings, or review quantities. An unproven but surprisingly valid rule of thumb, the Pareto Principle, suggests that 20 percent of your products are responsible for 80 percent of your profit.[77] Some experts argue that even 20 percent is generous.[78] The Principle is valid mostly to prompt you to find out for yourself. Run the data.

---

[76] Clausell, Tristan. "The Best Kept Secrets of Amazon's Private Labeling Initiative," Skubana, April 20, 2016, http://skubana.com/amazon-updates/the-best-kept-secrets-of-amazons-amazonbasics/

[77] "How to Analyse Your Business Sales — 80/20 Rule," The Chartered Institute of Marketing, www.cim.co.uk/files/8020rule.pdf

[78] "Five steps for achieving peak profitability with the 80/20 rule," Forté One, http://www.forteone.com/5-steps-for-achieving-peak-profitability-with-the-8020-rule/

> # 80/20:
> The Pareto Principle, which suggests that the majority of outcomes (profits) flow from a minority of efforts (products).

If you have dud products, develop "up or out" plans or discontinue them. If the rule of thumb is even close, they're probably already draining resources best used for protecting your winners.

8. Move down the long tail.
The future seems as clear as ever: As soon as any category and product within it is successful, Amazon will increasingly reach for a piece. In a market with a very long tail, they'll bite on the high-volume head of the demand curve.

Don't forget you always have the opportunity to shuffle toward the tail, which is *really* long. Known demand is a good thing, but stay away from products with immense volumes. Choose lesser-known, specialized products and market niches that haven't yet (and may never) attract Amazon's attention.

9. Diversify your sales channels.
Remember, Amazon is one distribution channel — admittedly, an important one, but not the only game in town.

Make sure your business plan includes some combination of your own web storefront and other channels, whether an established online marketplace like eBay, another Amazon geography without that Amazon branded competition, or a new, rising competitor. Depending on your products, you may even find that other channels can be more profitable.

> ## 73% of Amazon sellers
> also sell through eBay, and a majority expect to expand to a marketplace they're not already in.[79]

10. Make decisions from data.

Any successful seller must be nimble, ready to adapt for changing technologies, trends, economic conditions, and consumer taste, among dozens of other variables. Amazon invasion of your sales space is just one example.

Instead of reacting emotionally, lean on data. Get the tools you need for cause and effect analysis, comparisons, and tests of success. With such data, steer your business accordingly— by changing or diversifying your product mix, improving or extending your service, even exploring emerging business models such as freemium products. Such insight and agility is crucial for long-term success.

---

[79] *The State of the Amazon Marketplace 2016*, Feedvisor and WebRetailer, http://fv.feedvisor.com/stateofamazon.html

Chapter 9 —
Troubleshooting

In this section:

- How to troubleshoot PPC ads and keywords
- How to work with Seller Performance
- How to work with Seller Support
- How to get troubleshoot listing problems
- How to get a listing unlocked
- How to resurrect invisible listings
- How to thwart a hijacked listing
- How to handle a hazmat review
- How to troubleshoot FBA issues
- How to ensure you're treated fairly when FBA goods are returned
- How to troubleshoot customer feedback issues
- How to handle VAT invoice requests

How to troubleshoot PPC ads and keywords

As you've figured out by now, getting the flywheel moving and keeping it humming is largely about identifying what you believe are good keywords, using them as bait to catch more good ones, and then advertising with a set of the best to increase relevance and, hopefully, sell products.

Along the way, analyze each step of the sales funnel — from impressions to page views to sales — to identify anywhere you're losing shoppers. Troubleshoot at that stage; the appropriate responses depend on where in the funnel you're losing them.

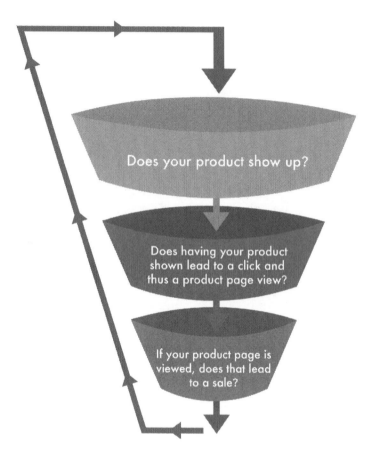

Meanwhile, your competitors are doing the same thing around you, so the results will be constantly shifting. Ultimately, track what matters: which keywords produce a strong organic search ranking for your product. Strive to move up in that search ranking — or at least not let competitors slip ahead.

Problem: No impressions

How can you get your ad shown more frequently when it's relevant?

Answer: There are a lot of conspiracy theories about a lack of impressions, but in our experience, if Amazon just won't show the ad, there are three and only three potential causes:

- The product is not in the top five subcategories for that keyword, so Amazon has deemed it not relevant to the keyword. (To check, enter the keyword in the search field and review the first five sub categories.) This problem mostly arises with new products, when Amazon is still assessing your product page and determining where your product should live. If you're convinced you should be in one of those top five but aren't, create a support request for it. Otherwise, find another keyword.
- You've neglected to include the keyword somewhere in your product page or hidden keyword fields. (It has to be in the indexed product keywords *and* your campaign.)
- You didn't bid high enough. If you do — probably well above what Amazon suggests would be a winning bid — the ad will eventually be shown. Then you'll get data about clicks and sales, too. If those are low, the keyword isn't relevant (enough) for your product. If you do make sales, however, relevance will be assigned, and you'll start getting more impressions, too.

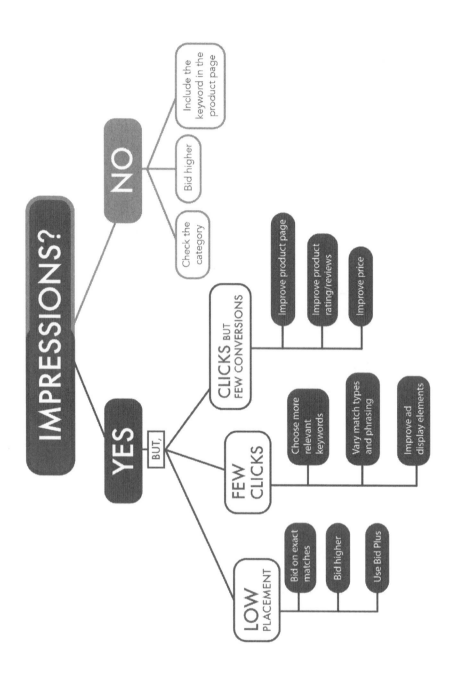

Problem: Your bids aren't winning top placement

It doesn't do you a whole lot of good to have an ad that doesn't appear before the third or fourth results page. What do you have to do to move it nearer the top?

Answer: Look at one of several possible explanations and the appropriate response:

- Bid on exact matches, which always defeat broader matches, even those with higher bids. In fact, determining the most effective keywords and bidding on exact matches for them, as described in the section on getting the flywheel moving, is a good way to optimize your advertising spend and spend less overall than many competitors who overpay for broader keywords. That doesn't mean you shouldn't use phrase matching, too, but if you're not winning placement, your phrase-match keywords may be too broad or too weak. Make them more specific or replace them with exact-match bids.

- Bid higher. Don't go by Amazon's "estimated first-page bid," which is misleadingly low.

- Use Bid Plus. Period. Amazon's support information makes it sound like you could get to the top of the first page without it, but in fact, it's a pre-requisite. You may get to somewhere on the first page without it, but you'll never receive the top placement.

Problem: Your ad is getting impressions, but you're not getting many clicks.

Low click-through could be a symptom of several problems.

Answer: The fundamental issue with low click-through is that when shoppers see the ad, they conclude that the product not what they're looking for. To solve this problem:

- Avoid impressions with shoppers who are actually searching for other types of products by ensuring your ad keywords are truly relevant. Specifically, add more relevant keywords to the campaign, with variations in match type and phrasing, and reduce your bids on questionable keywords with very low click-through.

- Ensure that the aspects of the product that display in the ad — the primary product image, title, product rating, and price— aren't turning off customers. If you're certain your keywords are relevant, work individually on each of those four elements to make your product, and thus your ad, more attractive.

Problem: Shoppers are clicking on ads to view your product page, but not buying.
How do you handle the worst-case scenario for PPC advertising — paying for clicks that don't convert?

Answer: Give more attention to your product page and price. You may need to do one or more of three things:

- Get critical eyes on your product information: Is it clear and with easy-to-find details about the features customers want? See the section of this guide on setting up product listings for guidance.
- Make sure you've got plenty of positive product reviews. See the sections of this guide on product and seller reviews.
- Ensure your price is right. Study the competition and consider lowering your price, at least for a time, to see if that makes the difference. Nobody wants a race to the bottom, but something about your product is turning shoppers off.

How to work with Seller Performance

Dealing with Seller Performance can be fraught, since it often involves scary issues like account suspension. Don't give them a reason to contact you, unless it's to celebrate your great sales and offer some of the semi-secret perks provided to top sellers. Thoroughly understand Amazon policies so you don't violate them. Monitor your performance metrics and act proactively to prevent things from ever getting that bad. (Be sure to stay up to date on the current metrics and targets, which are tweaked fairly often.)

If you follow this advice and the other recommendations in this guide, you're less to hear from Seller Performance about problems. That said, Amazon can be capricious, and suspensions seem to be on the rise, although more for resellers than for private label sellers. You may receive notice of any of these major problems:

- Account suspension
- Listing suspension
- FBA participation suspension

If Seller Performance does contact you with bad news — about off-target performance found in a review or with a warning or immediate suspension — follow the steps below for your best chance of surviving intact.

1. Calmly figure out what you've done wrong (or could do better).
Stick to facts, not emotions. Re-read notifications without the filters of surprise and emotion. Amazon notifications can be vague, perhaps by design, since they want you to do the work of scrutinizing your processes and telling them how you can improve. This can be very frustrating for sellers, but the best way to protect a business you care about is to ignore the lack of respect and communication, remember that "what Amazon gives, Amazon can take away," and move forward with practical steps toward resolution. That begins with identifying something to fix.

You should be aware of any performance issues already. A policy violation can be harder to identify specifically, but more so if you don't know the policies (and their implications) in the first place. Review your account and identify anything and everything that might be causing the objection.

Seller forums are a good place to read about typical problems, and examples can also be found on the relevant Amazon seller help page at http://tinyurl.com/h68qa4w.

2. Consider professional help.

Several consultants provide support for suspensions and other serious matters. Their experience and perspective may help, as long as you can enlist them quickly enough.

3. Act as quickly as you can without panicking.

Any kind of suspension can devastate a thriving business and destroy all momentum, and the longer your case sits, the less incentive anyone has to change the status quo. So drop everything and get your ducks in a row, ideally within a day or two. A prompt response helps convince them you're on top of your business and responsive to customers, too.

4. Create a case for a change.

Develop a remediation (or appeal) plan that addresses any and all of the things that may have caused the problem, even if you're not certain what that was. Explain *specifically* what you'll do to improve your operation broadly, including correcting issues and preventing them from happening again. Specify the timeframe you'll use. (Sixty days is the formal grace period for demonstrable improvement.) Document this plan of action in writing.

You may have gotten a warning about something you're not actually doing — suspected counterfeit products, for example. Many suspensions seem to be the result of a misunderstanding or poor judgment on Amazon's part. In that case, simply state your case and provide your evidence. But also consider whether the product or action that drew the red flag is worth defending again in the future or might best be avoided — a decision you also can document in your action plan.

5. Present your plan in a calm and collaborative tone.

Email is the only way to respond to Seller Performance notifications, probably to prevent sellers from shouting. Craft your email professionally. Resist the urge to make excuses, ask for exceptions, plead, or worst of all, threaten. Amazon has the power in this relationship, not you, and accepting that might as well be part of the terms of service. As an anonymous former support associate recently posted on an informative Reddit thread, "It frustrates me that many sellers approach selling on Amazon as if it were a fundamental human

right." (See http://www.reddit.com/r/FulfillmentByAmazon/
comments/3naqe8/i_am_a_former_seller_support_associate.)

Swallow your frustration, demonstrate humility, and convince the
person reading your appeal that something significant and practical
will change. Present your full plan of action in the spirit of working
together to solve a problem in a way that will benefit Amazon
customers.

6. Submit all supporting documentation at once.
You're probably only to get one chance; make it count. Provide
everything you can the first time.

7. Cross your fingers.
Sit tight while the process plays out. Don't prod; Seller Performance
uses an email queue rather than a ticketing system, so it's difficult for
additional contacts to successfully reference and be linked with the
original communication. Besides, signs of impatience may increase the
chances that you won't like the result.

8. If necessary, keep trying.
Subsequent contacts to Seller Performance, including revised Plans of
Action, carry long odds. But if you remain professional, you probably
have nothing to lose, and it may be necessary if you never get a
response the first time. The final option of escalating to Amazon CEO
Jeff Bezos should be reserved for a last-ditch attempt, only after
you've not only assessed the problem on your side but solved it.[80]

How to work with Seller Support
As with Seller Performance, there's an art to dealing with this Amazon
team, though the interactions are far more routine and less fraught. The
most common issues that require help from Seller Support include:

---

[80] McCabe, Chris, "Bezos Escalations: Then and Now," Seller Labs, Sept. 14, 2015,
http://www.sellerlabs.com/blog/bezos-escalations-then-and-now/

- Categories that have changed with unpleasant results. See the chapter on creating product listings for details about monitoring for, and addressing, category changes.
- Listing problems, of which there can be many, some of which may be your fault. See later in this chapter for specific tips.
- Holds on funds, which can occur if your product enjoys a sudden spike in volume. Amazon's anti-fraud practices include what's called a velocity review. While they make sure nothing fishy is going on, you won't get paid all you're due; they'll hold those funds in reserve to ensure they're not needed to cover refunds or claims. There's not much you can do about this, other than recognize that many new sellers go through it when sales take off. It's usually fairly quick, sufficient working capital should keep it from pinching too much, and in individual situations, providing appropriate documentation can help speed it up. Velocity reviews can take longer if your service metrics aren't up to snuff, so make sure they are.
- FBA problems, which can include a host of difficulties, from slow deliveries to lost shipments. See later in this chapter for tips.
- ASIN hijacking. See later in this chapter for specific tips.

Whether you need to request an additional category for your product or permission to enter a restricted category, following these steps can help improve the outcomes.

1. Be prepared.
Do your research before contacting Seller Support. For requests such as a change in category, do what you can to demonstrate your side of the story with rational and customer-focused information.

2. Consider the appropriate contact method.
Use the complexity of the issue and need for documentation to help decide whether to request a contact by email — so you'll have a clear paper trail — or by phone, when a dialogue might actually resolve things more quickly.

Tip: Consider your time zone.
Seller Support will either email or call you, per your request on their webform. The time zone you suggest for a call back could help or hinder you from a language perspective, particularly if your issue is complex. If your request is for North American business hours, you're more likely to get a North American support agent, and the same is true of Asian hours and agents. Aim for an hour when your preferred language is most likely to be native.

---

3. Stay professional.

Use Amazon terms and references when you can, since they'll understand more quickly what you're on about.

Resist the urge to complain, exaggerate the drama, or get testy. Seller Support is there to help you, but they're human, and nobody reacts well to abuse, threats, or muttering about anti-Amazon petitions or the Better Business Bureau. Calmly ask for help in solving the problem, and explain how the solution will benefit Amazon customers.

4. Be concise and focus on one issue per contact.

Present your case thoroughly but succinctly. Seller Support reps are as busy as you are and won't have the time or patience to hunt for the pertinent information. Plus, case numbers will be assigned by Seller Support for proactive requests, and since the issues may be resolved by different teams at Amazon, it'll only confuse and slow things to have multiple issues under the same case number.

5. Submit all supporting documentation at once.

Don't wait for them to ask. Resolve requests or issues with the fewest possible contacts by providing everything you can up front.

6. Be patient.

Seller Support is a large, multi-national, multi-tiered team in a big, decentralized organization, and it'd be almost impossible for any given associate to know everything. In addition, multiple Amazon teams, including the product catalog or FBA teams, may hold the answers or need to weigh in. That means complex tickets can be challenging to resolve and require Seller Support to open separate tickets, internally, with those teams.

When you know your request may take help from such groups, include in your initial request a statement of the problem in the terms those other teams will understand. You can even suggest to the first-line support agent that, for instance, "You may need to open a ticket with the catalog team, because the browse node on this ASIN was abandoned and we need to know what to do as a result."

Then let the process play out. Don't make the same request multiple times before hearing back from the first; it's likely to slow the response. Individually, support agents have a lot of power to implement solutions, but the fastest solution isn't necessarily the right one, and without guidance and time, lower-level agents often choose the fastest — which can cause problems later. (See the section below about locked listings for an example.)

7. If you don't get the answer you want, try again.
The performance metrics for Seller Support clearly favor fast response and resolution, which is fine unless you have a relatively complex issue — in which case, the agent almost certainly won't read and digest everything the first time. So the first response may be very cursory. (In their defense, like most customer support teams, they probably handle plenty of "Is it plugged in?" sorts of issues — and there's no question that their incremental support ticket system processes thousands of tickets a minute.)

So try again. You may simply get a different agent who knows more about your particular issue because they've seen it before. You can also ask to escalate. Seller Support is a tiered organization, with team leads and managers, and higher-ups include technical account managers, who are generally more tenured and able to handle tougher issues correctly.

8. Keep an eye on related listings and inventory afterward.
The system is complex, and the Law of Unintended Consequences suggests that sooner or later, in fixing one thing for you, Seller Support

will accidentally break something else, from re-locking a listing to incorrectly marking inventory as unfulfillable. The more products and listings you manage, the more you risk a problem going unnoticed, and the longer it persists, the harder it may be to fix later. (In addition, of course, are lost sales you'll never make up.)

Check up on inventory accuracy, listing validity, the arrival of funds due to you, and as many other aspects of the business as you feasibly can. Tools that are independent of, or at least in addition to, Seller Central reports can help flag variances between your view of reality and Amazon's.

How to troubleshoot listing problems

Maybe you've pulled up your product page and thought, "What the hell?" Or maybe you can't find it at all! The problems that befall product listings include:

- Broken listings, including the wrong images or outdated product information or pricing.
- Locked listings that won't permit you to make valid updates (including updates to correct problems noted above). This can be a daily headache for sellers with frequent specification or compatibility updates.
- Invisible listings — those that don't appear in a direct search, either as a result of an SEO issue or an intentional Amazon suspension of the listing.

These problems can be due to some error on your part, including not signing up for Brand Registry, so that another seller can contribute to the page. They can also be caused by Amazon intentionally or unintentionally updating the product page from its own information sources, such as Amazon Warehouse Deals — or even a well-meaning customer who's contacted Customer Support to "fix" what they perceive as wrong or misleading product information.

Listing problems can be a knot to untangle. Start here:

How to get a listing unlocked

If you can't update your listing with newer information, even if you're the manufacturer of record in the Brand Registry, your listing has been effectively locked.

All this really means is that someone with more authority than you is pulling rank. Listings can be updated by multiple product information sources, including Amazon's support teams, other sellers, and Amazon retail (because you provide them via Vendor Central) or the Amazon Warehouse. Various sources are considered more authoritative than others, and Amazon sources seem to trump even Brand Registry sellers. As a result, if Amazon updates a listing without outdated information or a lousy product photo, for instance, you may not be able to correct it without help from Seller Support.

1. Try to identify the source of conflicting information.

It's easy enough to go to Amazon Warehouse Deals or any other seller's page and figure out if it's their ugly iPhone shot that's replaced all your professional and carefully orchestrated images.

2. If your products appear in Amazon Warehouse Deals, consider buying them out.

Some sellers scoop up those discounted products simply to get Amazon off the product listing. That may help prevent unwanted "contributions" to the product page that override yours.

3. Contact Seller Support.

Provide the correct or new information, along with your evidence that you own the brand.

But don't settle for a manual override, if you can help it. Be specific not only about the correction but about what needs to happen to fix it. If you rush the support rep, they may manually override the listing with your new information, in part because that's the path of least resistance. But it isn't the right one, and it would mean that next time you have a product spec change, the page will (still) be locked, and you'll soon have numerous products you can't update without new support tickets each time.

4. Get the conflicting input source removed.

It won't be as quick, but the real solution is to ask the rep to take the necessary steps to identify where the conflicting input came from, if necessary, and, if possible, to remove it. That way, the listing will revert back to your control and you can update it in the usual fashion, without contacting Seller Support each time.

How to resurrect invisible listings

Has your product vanished? It's not alien abduction. Page suppression and sudden burial in the search results can both be a problem that can cause product death.

1. Check your Seller Central pages.

In most cases, intentionally suppressed listings will be flagged, with a reason you can address and discuss with Seller Central.

The trickier problem is when the listing is not fully suppressed but shows up on page 120 of the search results, with lots of irrelevant things ahead of it. The cause can be tough to sniff out, since there's no visual evidence of what's wrong. Review all of your performance metrics and make sure nothing's wrong there that is disadvantaging your product in the search algorithm.

2. Not FBA? Reconsider.

FBA sellers are prioritized by numerous Amazon algorithms, so if you're not a participant, that will always be a factor in search results.

3. Check that your category hasn't changed.

Confirm the validity of your keywords for that category (including search attempts with potential negative keywords). If that's okay, too, it could be that events or competitor actions — including a stockout on your part or big price changes elsewhere — have zapped the energy from your flywheel.

4. Try to spin the flywheel.
Poke around and see what competitors are doing. Then give your product a little love and drive traffic to it through advertising or external promotion. If your listing doesn't rise in the results as you might expect (which is admittedly subjective), move to the next step.

5. Reassess your whole product listing, including keywords.
Use your attempts at advertising to analyze keyword reports. Are your keywords aligned with what people really search for? Is your price? Are your photos lousy? The ads you tried in the previous step help because they'll give you lots of data about clicks, views, and sales, and may reveal the problem.

6. Make sure you're using all the data points in your schema.
If you still haven't found the problem, buckle in; the other things that may be quietly broken can drive you insane.

Each major product browse node has its own XML schema, including specific fields for sometimes hundreds of data points that may or may not apply to your specific product. This data is used, for instance, in the filters customers can use to narrow search results. Certainly not all may be relevant to your product, but the more of them you can fill in, the better. Leaving them blank can hurt search results.

7. If all else fails, contact Seller Support.
Share whatever you've been able to learn and see if they can shed any light on the issue. This may sometimes include recent changes on their side that may have had unintentional results.

How to thwart a hijacker
Successful private label products can attract the attention of counterfeiters. These bad actors may include a slightly twisted version of your company or product name in their listings, hoping to capitalize with unwary shoppers looking for your product. More often, even though you participate in the Brand Registry, unethical sellers may get a sample of your product to study it, arrange for its manufacture, and

then offer their copycat product — almost certainly with a lower price and probably lower quality — on your listing. This problem is also known as ASIN hijacking or piggybacking, and it can be tricky to recognize before lost sales, returns, and negative feedback start adding up. This problem has caused several high-profile brands to refuse to participate in the Amazon marketplace at all.

To prevent a mass exodus, Amazon has been transitioning toward providing more support and protection to private-label sellers and brands. That has meant getting more serious about hosting quality sellers with quality products rather over emphasizing price via a horde of resellers. The resultant "brand gating" has expanded the product categories that require permission to enter and started charging authorized third-party sellers a substantial one-time fee to sell certain brands on the site. Those entry barriers should help reduce hijacking and well-meaning but unauthorized resellers.

Although the narrowing of brand gates is not likely over, now is probably a better time than ever to be a private-label seller. Unethical sellers are likely to still find a way to abuse you, but if so, there are steps you can take to combat it.

1. Be sure your product images include your branding.
Try to set up your main product image (and any images that include your packaging) so that your brand name or logo is clearly visible. This is a preventive measure like locking your doors: It won't stop all the bad guys, but it's likely to send most to an easier target.

2. Watch for spikes in returns or negative product feedback.
Sudden problems can also indicate a defect in a shipment, of course. But regardless of the cause, you need to figure out the problem and fix it, and when it isn't the product itself or your presentation of it, it could be that a hijacker's product is tarring your reputation.

3. Keep an eye on your buy box and "other sellers on Amazon."
It's legitimate for someone who buys your product to offer it (with your permission) for resale at a price that reflects some wholesale or

bulk discount. It's also legitimate for anyone to offer it in used condition.

If you don't authorize resale on Amazon, and the product's offered as new, you should be the only seller. (Even if you do sell wholesale, you could make a prohibition against online resale a condition of the sale. You also may want to keep track of who's buying and in what quantities to ensure that you're not selling wholesale to a competitor. That way, should a problem arise, you can rule out any legitimate sellers... or stop selling to them. Because you may lose the buy box if other sellers, legitimate or not, sell your new products for a lower price than you do. This includes Amazon, and is one reason you may not want to open the can of worms known as Vendor Central.)

4. Consider having an employee or friend buy the hijacking product.
It may be painful to give the counterfeiter even one sale, but having it in hand with its packaging is probably the easiest way to confirm that it's fake.

It's not unheard of for factories — or middlemen working with them — to knowingly or mistakenly sell a product contracted exclusively to you to other sellers or even Amazon itself, so you may also find that it's not fake or lower quality at all, but simply your product imprinted with someone else's brand. In that case, you'll need to contact your factory and persuade them to stop.

5. Identify the seller and send a polite but clear message to cut it out.
Include references to your brand rights, trademarks, Amazon policy, and perhaps the applicable federal trade laws. A fair number of counterfeiters who know they're cheating won't press their luck but will simply remove their items. And some don't seem to realize it's both unethical and illegal.

Technically, Amazon prohibits communication between sellers, but a polite email or letter under the radar is usually effective and tends to work better than threatening letters from attorneys (if you can even find a physical or snail mail address to use). Indicate that you'd hate to get Amazon involved, but that you will if necessary.

6. If that doesn't work, contact Seller Support.
Counterfeiting violates policy and can get seller accounts suspended. Provide your evidence of the fake and copies of any communication with the other seller.

How to handle a hazmat review
Even if your product doesn't qualify as a hazardous material or contain potentially hazardous components such as magnets or batteries, you still may receive notice of a hazmat review, either for a new product you're trying to list or one in an Amazon shipment or warehouse. Speed the process by being prepared in advance.

1. Keep updated MSDS on file as part of your product and supplier documentation.
Most manufacturers are familiar with material safety data sheets (MSDS) requirements and can provide them on request for any component materials in your products. You might even want to make clear, efficient MSDS access part of your supplier selection processes.

2. Submit additional documentation to Amazon promptly when requested.
This should include an ingredients list and any raw material information or safety validation from the manufacturer, as well as any applicable MSDS. If no MSDS exists for your product or its materials, you may need to complete an MSDS exemption form, depending on your product category. Amazon provides the exemption form and examples on the relevant help page at http://tinyurl.com/hsaqt7z.

3. Keep your MSDS exemption sheets on file, too.
They can help you quickly provide the required information for any new but similar products in the future.

4. Prevent future problems by providing all hazmat information when listing.
If a review determines that your inventory is more hazardous than Amazon or a shipper can handle, it'll be destroyed, not shipped back to you. Avoid this costly possibility by fully understanding hazmat restrictions and providing all necessary information to Amazon when you create a product listing and prior to shipping any inventory.

How to troubleshoot FBA issues
Although FBA is a wise choice for most private-label sellers, it doesn't come without headaches. Sometimes in the millions of items shuffled by Amazon warehouses, products get mislabeled or lost, items that aren't supposed to be commingled end up that way, inventory is mysteriously marked unfulfillable, returns get put back into inventory without a quality or parts check, and sellers get inventory noncompliance warnings that aren't accurate.

1. Did we mention Brand Registry?
Another argument for applying to the Brand Registry is that, since you then own the UPC or other unique product identifier, you eliminate the need to manually label your products for shipment to Amazon (other than the manufacturing UPC or identifier barcode). Since the correct scanning of manual labels seem to be a source of problems, that's a quick end-run around them.

2. Make sure your options for returns handling are what you want.
Unless your shipments are unusually small and you have plenty of lead time, don't use Amazon's "inventory placement service," where you ship to one warehouse and they distribute internally as they see fit. In addition to the fee, it can take longer than necessary for those items to become available for sale and internal transfers increase the risk of problems. Stick with the default, distributed inventory placement, which requires you to ship to separate warehouses yourself.
If you're selling in a category that allows it, commingled inventory typically isn't a source of problems for alert Brand Registry sellers, and it does make it easier to track inventory globally.

Repackaging is another matter. If you have a product that gets quality assurance testing before shipment or involves parts that a customer might inadvertently or intentionally leave out of the box when returning it, avoid having a faulty or incomplete product shipped to a second customer by being sure your FBA settings do not give permission for repackaging.

Some sellers have suffered incidents when this setting seems to be ignored, but for the most part, you can prevent passing a problem product along to a new customer — and the feedback and reputation damage that results — by removing the option.

3. Help prevent human error when you can.
Mistakes will happen, but try to make life easy for warehouse staff. If you do label products rather than simply using a UPC or other unique identifier, ensure those labels are correct, readily visible, and in the same place on all packaging to help avoid any need to re-label at the warehouse, which can take weeks (in which case your product will not be available for sale).

When feasible, help mistake-proof the process by using different shipments or containers (or pallets) for different ASINs. If you sell items in case packs, indicate that right on the case. Similarly, don't tempt anyone to take shortcuts like scanning one barcode or label for multiple items that look alike but aren't; separate them by shipments or take other measures to ensure that every item gets scanned as it's supposed to.

4. Keep detailed inventory and shipment records.
This can help you check up on and resolve issues with your carrier as well as with Amazon. If you do need to contact Seller Support, be prepared to offer evidence, including photographic evidence when feasible, of what you sent, where, and when.

How to ensure you're treated fairly when FBA goods are returned

Refunds for returned FBA inventory are FBA-related issues that sometimes need more management than they should.

When customers request refunds for reasons unrelated to a product problem, typically Amazon immediately gives the customer a refund and withholds (or debits) the funds due for the sale, but may wait until the item has been returned to a warehouse to credit the seller with the inventory. If the item never comes back, by policy, Amazon takes the loss by issuing the seller a refund. (Then, if the item does eventually show up, Amazon appears to keep it and sell it through Amazon Warehouse Deals.) Different categories have slightly different return timeframes, but generally the seller credits are supposed to be made within 45 days of the refund request.

Recently, refunds have been delayed or sometimes overlooked completely. As a result, sellers are out both the sale and the inventory item. Be sure to get all the funds that you're due:

1. Audit your return credits.
You may need a tool to track refunded orders for which you haven't been paid.

Commercial tools are available specifically for this purpose, some of which also audit related items such as restocking fees or inventory damaged in transit. At least one of these tools costs nothing but a percentage of the amount recovered — a business model that alone suggests how much money you could be due.

2. Submit a list of overdue refunds to Seller Support.
When you request reimbursement with specific information about the refunded orders, inventory transactions (or lack thereof), and dates, they're pretty good about checking the backtrail and either issuing the refund or pointing out where the appropriate credits have already been made.

How to troubleshoot customer feedback issues

Unfortunately, seller and product feedback doesn't always go smoothly. As discussed in the feedback chapters of this guide, there's a lot you can do to prevent damaging reviews, but you still may face issues such as:

- Negative seller feedback when the fault is an FBA issue.
- Seller or product feedback that contains offensive language or is incomprehensible.
- Misplaced or mistaken feedback that clearly relates to some other product or seller.
- Feedback that has nothing to do with the product, perhaps left by someone who hasn't purchased or used it. (See sidebar).
- Fraudulent feedback that you suspect was left by a competitor.
- Multiple negative reviews by the same customer.

Here's how to address them:

1. Know Amazon policies about feedback.

Stay familiar with Amazon's policies about feedback, both as laid out for sellers and described for customers, which emphasize different details. That way, you can refer to the Amazon policy being violated when requesting removals — and avoid wasting time by asking for removal of reviews that you may not like but that Amazon is unlikely to delete.

2. Try first to resolve issues directly with the customer.

Amazon's Feedback Manager can help you do this for seller feedback that's negative or clearly was left in error. For a negative product review, you'll need a buyer/review matching tool to associate the review with an order and thus the customer. See the seller and product review chapters for more details and options, including offering a replacement product and asking (politely) for editing or removal of the offending review.

3. Get FBA-related seller feedback stricken.

As noted in the seller feedback chapter, customers may leave negative feedback that's really a problem introduced by Amazon FBA. Seller

Support is good about striking out that feedback, accepting the blame, and removing the score from your average metrics. Simply contact them and point out the issue, with evidence regarding the FBA status of the product that prompted the review.

4. Provide supporting evidence when asking for removal of reviews that violate policy.

When feedback doesn't follow Amazon's policies, request its removal. Include a clear argument for what's wrong and why it should be fixed, including reviewer identities and any evidence you may have that feedback is being posted by a competitor, includes multiple reviews on the same product by the same person, cut-and-paste repetitions, etc. Refer to the Amazon policy being violated.

5. Consider the advantages and disadvantages of a public response.

For negative feedback in a customer review that complies with policy, decide whether you can respond to the comment publicly in a way that helps more than it hurts, given that responding may actually raise the visibility of or validate silly feedback. See the customer and product feedback for more tips and preventive measures.

How to handle VAT invoice requests

Taxes are complicated, and VAT is one of the tough ones.

If you have a European Union company and therefore a Value Added Tax (VAT) registration number, you probably already know the ins and outs of VAT charges, exemptions, and invoice requests. Enter your VAT registration number when you set up your seller account, and have at it.

If your company is elsewhere and you want to sell via Amazon's EU marketplaces — and you do — you'll need to get cozy with VAT because you'll owe it to the authorities in either the countries where you inventory or, once you pass certain sales thresholds, ship to. (There are some minor exceptions, but they're unlikely to apply to most successful private-label sellers.) Plus, European customers often expect a VAT invoice, which is frequently required by law when requested. This is because VAT is collected in stages at every point in the distribution cycle — everywhere value is added — and those who have paid VAT with the intention of reselling the product are eligible for that amount as a credit against their own VAT liability later.

The VAT could consume a book chapter by itself, but in general:

1. Don't miss out on sales in the UK or Europe simply because VAT is daunting.
It's worth figuring out. And at least until the Brexit decision changes Britain's official EU standing, you can use Amazon's multi-country (EFN) fulfillment deal to ship inventory to just one country, such as England, and still sell to the other European countries with Amazon marketplaces. That simplifies the VAT issues, at least to start, while your sales are still under certain thresholds.

2. Request a VAT registration number.
Record this number with Amazon as soon as your inventory lands at an FBA fulfillment center in Europe. The details and rates vary based on the country where the inventory resides. You can get one in the UK, along with some education, at www.gov.uk/vat-businesses. Once you have it, enter it in the appropriate field in your seller account information with Amazon.

3. Understand your VAT obligations.
If you're using FBA, as is generally wise, you'll need to charge VAT on your sales, file the appropriate tax returns and pay VAT amounts due to the various tax authorities, and provide VAT invoices on request. Tracking and reporting VAT amounts paid to you by order — not to mention keeping tabs on your own VAT liability — can be time-consuming. It's one place an automated tool can save time and effort.

If your product is FBM instead and you're storing your inventory locally and shipping individual orders across borders, different requirements can apply. Still, you are typically responsible for meeting any VAT obligations that apply, often as soon as the products are imported. Import VAT payments will be credited against the amount of VAT owed upon sale.

4. Talk to an expert before diving in.

Because they vary by EU member country and sometimes by product type, these VAT issues are complicated. You can start with Amazon's overview, which includes a few helpful webinar links, but you'll also need to talk to an experienced tax advisor. (See http://tinyurl.com/z92d9h3.)

5. When a customer requests a VAT invoice, provide one.

Generate an electronic or paper copy of the invoice with the VAT taxes you charged the customer as a line item. If you didn't tack on the tax as an additional fee, VAT is treated as though included in the sales price, so you'll need to work backwards to indicate the nominal product price and the amount of the total that accounts for VAT.

If a customer in a far-off place ordered a product from the U.S. marketplace and you shipped it to them FBM across borders as a one-off, without having a VAT registration number, you probably didn't charge the tax and the customer was responsible for any import taxes or duties, including VAT. (But we don't advise this approach; the shipping is expensive, it's not scalable, and you're flirting with legal issues, depending on the country.) If that customer asks for a VAT invoice, simply send a copy spelling out that no VAT was charged.

You can get software or other automation tools to help with VAT accounting, invoice, and reporting software.

Tool Description: VAT Invoice Automation Tool

If you sell in Europe, you know that VAT invoice generation can be a complicated and time-consuming task. With Efficient Era's VAT Invoice Tool you could either automate the process of creating and sending VAT invoices to every customer who makes a purchase, or chose to send them a link to a VAT invoice generation form that they fill out.

Earning your troubleshooter merit badge

The longer you spend selling online, the more difficulties you may run into, since the rules of the game tend to change and with little or no notice. The challenges also tend to evolve in the constant tug-of-war between Amazon or other marketplace providers catching up with unethical sellers, and those sellers trying to find new ways around the rules.

As time passes and your experience grows, however, rest assured that you'll become an expert in helping Seller Support, Seller Performance, or other Amazon teams to help you.

Efficient Era

Glossary

ACOS: Advertising cost of sale. A metric by which you can determine whether the sales prompted by a pay-per-click ad campaign are worth the cost.

AmazonBasics: Amazon's in-house brand for products that range from household goods to electronics accessories. Consider AmazonBasics a competing brand.

Amazon Business: A buying option that enables sellers to attract customers interested in certifications, bulk discounts, purchase-order purchases, and other benefits of a B2B vendor relationship.

Amazon Prime: Amazon's paid shopper membership program, which provides free two-day shipping on eligible Amazon and FBA products, as well as other benefits such as free music or movies. Because customers tend to favor Amazon Prime products, you'll probably want your products to be eligible if possible. See also *Seller Fulfilled Prime*.

Amazon retail: The part of Amazon's business where it sells products made by others and, usually, purchased wholesale through either Vendor Central or Vendor Express. Sellers lose control of pricing, marketing, and other product management when participating in Amazon retail. (In public uses, the term may also refer to Amazon's retail stores in a half-dozen cities.)

Amazon Seller Central: See *Seller Central*. (Hey, we didn't want to put the whole glossary under "A." Just those Amazon terms that are concatenated words, like AmazonBasics, or that would be confusingly generic alone.)

AmazonSmile: An Amazon Marketplace platform alternative to www.amazon.com that allows users to select a charity that will receive a small percentage of their purchase amounts.

Amazon Giveaway: A promotional program in which an organization or individual buys Amazon products and uses the Amazon platform to distribute those products to giveaway participants in exchange for a social media following or other awareness activity. Some sellers may find it a useful promotional vehicle for their own products.

Amazon Warehouse Deals: See *Warehouse Deals*.

ASIN: Amazon Standard Identification Number. This 10-digit number is associated with a product listing, not the product per se, and can change. It may be used by other sellers of the same product.

ASIN hardening: An Amazon process that assembles what the algorithm considers the best titles, photos, feature text, and descriptions for any given product from the contributions of multiple sellers. ASIN hardening sounds good in theory and can be useful when many sellers are offering the same generic product, but it reduces the brand owner's control of private-label product listings, and it can result in locked listings that can't readily be updated with new information.

Basic selling plan: The U.K.'s version of the Individual selling plan, which is below the Professional selling plan status you probably want. The selling plans offer different fee structures and benefits.

Bid Plus: A new Amazon PPC advertising option in which a seller gives permission to spend 1.5 times their bid to get top positioning on the results page. It's impossible to win that top spot without it.

Brand Registry: Amazon's register of brands and brand owners, who gain more control over their product listings and some protection from counterfeiters by registering their ownership of their brand. Unless they're working in one of the few product categories that are ineligible, private-label sellers should apply for registration without delay.

Browse node: The Amazon terminology for a section in its hierarchical browse-tree structure. Browse nodes include root nodes, parent nodes, and leaf (or child) nodes. A root node aligns with a department and is typically named similarly.

BTG: Browse tree guide. The category and subcategory system for each Amazon root node (top-level department).

Certified Refurbished: A used item that has been refurbished and tested — by the manufacturer or, when applicable, by Amazon — and is being sold to work like new. They often include some warranty. The most examples are found in electronics and small appliance categories, but many other types of Certified Refurbished products are available, too.

Child node: See *browse node.*

Cold start: Amazon's term for the difficulty faced by new product listings, in which a lack of page traffic and sales means the product it remains buried in the search results... where it's difficult to draw clicks and sales. In effect, inertia keeps the flywheel from moving. It's a vicious cycle that can only be overcome by adding energy to the flywheel via advertising, other promotion, sales, and customer reviews.

Conversion rate: The rate at which shoppers who view your product page click buy buttons.

Department: Amazon's highest product categorization level, such as Automotive Parts and Accessories, Appliances, or Books.

EAN: Originally the acronym for European Article Number, which is now known as International Article Number. Like a UPC, an EAN is a unique identifier for product tracking, one with more international use. Also like UPCs, EAN barcodes may have various number of digits; EAN-13 is most common and is superset of the 12-digit UPC known as UPC-A.

FBA: Fulfillment by Amazon. You ship goods to Amazon in bulk and they handle shipment to individual customers, taking on much (though not all) of the fulfillment and customer service burden, including processing of returns. FBA participants are favored in search algorithms, and only FBA products are eligible for Amazon Prime. See also *Seller Fulfilled Prime*.

FBM: Fulfillment by merchant. Amazon brokers the sale and you ship directly to the customer, dealing with all related customer service, including returns. See also *Seller Fulfilled Prime*.

Flywheel effect: A flywheel is a mechanical device that uses principles of inertia and momentum to store energy and use it to maintain or increase speed. In online sales, the flywheel effect means that the more traffic you generate to your page, the easier it is to improve your product's discoverability, and the more sales you make, the easier it is to make more sales. See *virtuous cycle*.

GCID: Global Catalog Identification number. This permanent and unique, 16-digit number is assigned to products registered by manufacturers and private label sellers through the Amazon Brand Registry.

Individual selling plan: Amazon's basic selling plan, which is below the Professional selling plan status you probably want. The selling plans offer different fee structures and benefits.

Item type keyword: A type of keyword used only on Amazon.com that is related to, but more specific than, the product's browse node. Some nodes and categories have mandatory item types. They're optional or unavailable in others.

Keyword: A word or series of words (such as children's chewable vitamin) that online shoppers or other search engine users enter to search.

Leaf node: See *browse node*.

Locked listing: A product listing that you can't update, even though it's your product. Requires the involvement of Seller Support.

Negative keyword: A word or series of words that help search engines and algorithms exclude results that probably aren't what the shopper or search user is looking for. For instance, a useful negative keyword for an eyebrow pencil might be "school supplies." That way, if a shopper enters "makeup" and "pencil," a yellow #2 Ticonderoga with eraser won't appear at the top of the search results.

Node ID: The identifying number of a category or subcategory of the Amazon browse structure. Node IDs may have varying number of digits, with related IDs typically ending with, rather than beginning with, the same number. For instance, node IDs 2795108031 and 64348031 are both in the Beauty and Personal Care department. See also *browse node*.

Organic search: A search initiated by a shopper entering keywords. Organic search results are based on keywords and weighted by sales and other factors. Paid search results, on the other hand, are influenced by advertisers' bids on the keywords used by the shopper.

Parent node: See *browse node*.

Platinum seller: This invitation-only program is for large sellers with solid track records and outstanding sales and customer service metrics. It offers benefits that range from additional product keywords to better access to Amazon reps and support staff.

PPC: Pay per click. Google AdWords and Amazon Sponsored Products are notable examples.

Private-label: Branded. Private-label sellers are third-party sellers who sell (and usually design) their own branded products, usually in branded packaging. Private-label sellers are often contrasted with resellers, who are also third-party sellers but who participate in retail arbitrage to sell others' brand or unbranded products.

Professional seller: A participant in the upper tier of the seller plans for third-party resellers and private-label sellers. The lower level is known as Individual selling plan (in the U.S.) or Basic selling plan (in the U.K.). The selling plans offer different fee structures and benefits. See also *Platinum seller*.

Relevance: An assessment of how perfectly your product will match what the buyer is looking for. Relevance is a complex, black-box assessment based on category and keywords, sales ranking, reviews, price, and probably other data.

Removal order: The Amazon term for a request to "remove" goods from your inventory and ship them back to you (usually because the items have been returned, damaged, or otherwise are no longer sellable. But maybe just because you missed them).

Root node: A top-level category in the Amazon browsing structure, which typically aligns with and is named similarly to a department. See *browse node* and *department*.

Seller Central: The web portal that provides the dashboard you'll use to track sales and inventory and manage your relationship with Amazon and Amazon customers.

Seller Fulfilled Prime: An FBM option in which sellers with metrics over certain thresholds who can meet the Prime shipment guarantee can use the Prime flag regionally on select products, even though they're not FBA products.

Seller Support: The front-line Amazon team that (sometimes) helps with many seller issues, from locked listings to lost inventory shipments.

Seller Performance: The scary Amazon team that sends warnings about low performance (such as poor seller ratings) or policy violations. Sellers may need to work with this team to address listing or account suspensions or other business-threatening concerns.

Sponsored Products: An Amazon pay-per-click advertising program in which sellers bid on keywords; winning bids receive ad placement along with the organic results of searches on those keyword.

Super URL: Links to product pages that appear to contain search keywords and thus were once (but no longer) thought to boost product relevance for those keywords. By most interpretations, Amazon policies about manipulating product rankings would prohibit their use anyhow.

Third-party seller: Any seller on Amazon who is neither Amazon nor a manufacturer. In addition to private-label sellers, third-party sellers include many resellers engaging in retail arbitrage.

UPC: Uniform Product Code. UPCs are a unique product identification number that began in the U.S. grocery industry. (There's your trivia for the day.) UPCs currently come in two sizes; the 12-digit number and barcode format known as UPC-A is probably the most common. Like EANs, UPCs are used for product identification and tracking.

VAT: Value Added Tax. A tax on sales transactions at each level (e.g., wholesale, distribution, retail) that is due for most sales to European customers of online marketplaces.

Vendor Central: An invitation-only program in which you sell wholesale to Amazon, and they handle the sales, promotion, and customer service from there. Pros include some additional marketing opportunities and much lower demands on your management time;

cons include lower margins and loss of control over product pricing or much of anything else.

Vendor Express: A lower-commitment version of Vendor Central which doesn't require an invitation and can be explored on a trial basis (for both parties).

Verified Purchase: The Amazon flag on a product review that indicates the reviewer bought the product through Amazon for full price or no more than a 50 percent discount. Reviews without this flag are still valuable but can be viewed with more skepticism by shoppers.

Virtuous cycle: The opposite of a vicious cycle, that is, good things happen which makes more good things happen. See also flywheel effect.

Warehouse Deals: Amazon's "discount" product offers, many of which are returned products that are still new or like new. Some sellers dream about being able to opt out, since Warehouse Deals sometimes seem to be the source of faulty or incomplete products getting to customers, as well as outdated product information overwriting or locking current product listings.

About the Authors

Bernie Thompson

Bernie worked for 15 years as a software developer for IBM, S3, Microsoft, and DisplayLink and subsequently founded several start-ups before creating Plugable Technologies in 2009. After spending his career working on devices and device drivers, he recognized an opportunity to deliver higher quality, plug-and-play products while providing better customer support to succeed in channels, including Amazon, where product reviews matter. Plugable bet on Amazon and FBA from day one, succeeding in the brutal electronics category against big competitors. Spending the first year and a half doing everything himself motivated him to automate as much as possible, and Efficient Era was born in 2014 as a way to share the resulting tools with others. Bernie lives in the Seattle area with his family and dog and frequently hikes in the surrounding mountains.

Joni Sensel

Joni is the author or ghostwriter of more than half a dozen nonfiction books on topics ranging from feathers to Lean healthcare. She also writes fiction for young readers. She lives at the knees of Mt. Rainier with her sweetheart, two dogs, sundry elk, and the occasional mouse. Read more at www.jonisensel.com.

Printed in Great Britain
by Amazon